ST. PHOTIOS THE GREAT

Ἀπολυτίκια:

Ἦχος δ΄.

Ὠ'ς τῶν ἀποστόλων ὁμότροπος, καὶ τῆς οἰ-
κουμένης διδάσκαλος, τῷ Δεσπότῃ τῶν ὅλων
ἱκέτευε Φώτιε, εἰρήνην τῇ οἰκουμένῃ δωρήσα-
σθαι, καὶ ταῖς ψυχαῖς ἡμῶν τὸ μέγα ἔλεος.

Ἦχος πλ. α΄. Τὸν συνάναρχον Λόγον.

Τῆς σοφίας ἐκφάντωρ, λαμπρὸς γενόμενος,
Ὀρθοδοξίας ἐδείχθης θεοπαγὴς προμαχών, τῶν
πατέρων καλλονὴ Φώτιε μέγιστε· σὺ γὰρ αἱρέσεων δεινῶν,.στηλιτεύεις τὴν ὀφρύν, Ἑώας τὸ
θεῖον σέλας, τῆς Ἐκκλησίας λαμπρότης, ἣν δια-
τήρει πάτερ ἄσειστον.

Κοντάκιον

Ἦχος πλ. δ΄. Τῇ ὑπερμάχῳ.

Τῆς Ἐκκλησίας ὁ φωστὴρ ὁ τηλαυγέστατος,
καὶ ὀρθοδόξων ὁδηγὸς ὁ ἐνθεώτατος, στεφανού-
σθω νῦν τοῖς ἄνθεσι τῶν ἀσμάτων, ἡ θεόφθογ-
γος κιθάρα ἡ τοῦ Πνεύματος, ὁ στερρότατος
αἱρέσεων ἀντίπαλος, ᾧ καὶ κράζομεν· Χαῖρε
πάντιμε Φώτιε.

ST. PHOTIOS THE GREAT

ST. PHOTIOS THE GREAT

By

ASTERIOS GEROSTERGIOS

INSTITUTE FOR BYZANTINE
AND MODERN GREEK STUDIES
115 Gilbert Road
Belmont, Massachusetts 02178

Copyright © 1980, by Asterios Gerostergios
Published by THE INSTITUTE FOR BYZANTINE
AND MODERN GREEK STUDIES, INC.
115 Gilbert Road, Belmont, Massachusetts 02178, U.S.A.
Library of Congress Catalog Card Number: 80-82285
Printed in the United States of America

Clothbound ISBN 0-914744-50-X
Paperbound ISBN 0-914744-51-8

PREFACE

St. Photios the Great (820-891), Patriarch of Constantinople, was a great Orthodox spiritual and intellectual leader, the most important of his time, and truly a holy man. Yet his life and works are far from having received the attention they deserve. As a result, he has been seriously misunderstood and even maligned in the West. There is not a single work in English that gives a full and true picture of Photios' personality and contributions.

The present book by the Rev. Dr. Asterios Gerostergios, of the Greek Orthodox Church in America, comes to meet the need for such a work. In a clear, concise, and scholarly manner, Fr. Gerostergios deals in ten chapters with the origin of Photios, his education, the fruits of his education, his election to the Patriarchal throne of Constantinople, his first deposition and exile, his second Patriarchal reign, his second deposition and death, and the question of the role he played in the Schism between the Eastern Orthodox Church and the Western. Offering ample documentation for what he says, Fr. Gerostergios succeeds in establishing the lofty Christian character of Photios, the purity of his life, his many-sided greatness, and the groundlessness of the charge that Photios was the cause of the Schism between the East and the West.

Fr. Gerostergios has enhanced the value of his text by the addition at the end of many beautiful hymns, taken from the service in honor of St. Photios. These give vivid expression to the profound esteem which the Orthodox have for this illustrious Church Father.

St. Photios the Great is a very informative and edifying book. It deserves a wide audience.

Constantine Cavarnos

ACKNOWLEDGMENTS

The author of this volume wishes to express his deep gratitude and appreciation to the following individuals for their contribution in making possible its publication:

Dr. Norman Brown, for reading the first draft of the manuscript and offering valuable suggestions.

Professor Constantine Cavarnos, of Hellenic College, for reading the entire manuscript and making many improvements in expression. Dr. Cavarnos' help and encouragement were very instrumental in the appearance of this book in print.

Father Artemios, of the Kalyva "St. Savvas" at the Holy Mountain of Athos, for providing the photograph of an icon of St. Photios done at their Kalyva; and Mr. Basil Bacos, a student at Holy Cross Greek Orthodox School of Theology, for drawing the icon for the cover of the book.

The author gratefully acknowledges also the generous financial assistance given for the publication of this work by Mr. Christos Tsampouris; the Petrelis Family, in memory of John Petrelis and Eleni Petrelis; and Stavros Pappas, in memory of his mother-in-law Kleanthi Themistoklis.

Finally, I owe thanks to Cambridge University Press for permission to quote extensively from F. Dvornik's book *The Photian Schism*.

CONTENTS

INTRODUCTION

The ninth century constitutes one of the most turbulent periods of history. In this century such significant events took place that following generations of mankind were influenced and a new era of human history began. Thus, the spiritual streams and the evolution of human thought during the middle and modern ages find their sources in this century. Truly then, the ninth century constitutes a source of inspiration for intellectual men.

As is known, the first half of this century was still shaking from the Iconoclastic Controversy. The whole known world of that time in the East and the West participated in this struggle with all of its spiritual powers. Civilizing streams of the

classic, Hellenistic, Roman, and Christian antiquity which mingled with other streams coming
from the East were struggling with each other for
survival and domination in the future. As in
the first Christian centuries, Christianity clashed
against Greek thought and resulted in the Christian heresies which threw the Christian world
into confusion for many years. So also during the
ninth century and even earlier (from 726 to 843)
we observe a similar struggle of Christianity like
that of the past. While the characteristic points
of the struggle during the first five or six centuries
have been thoroughly examined and almost a
unanimous agreement has been reached by historians and scholars in general, the cause of the
gigantic contest of the spirit during the eighth
and ninth centuries still remains rather obscure
and there is a great deal of disagreement and difference of opinion among the various scholars.
Thus, some of the scholars claim that the struggle
had a Christological character, while others regard as its basis the awakening of the ancient
Greek spirit, which arose after the darkness of the
sixth and seventh centuries. Some others see the
cause of this conflict in the influence which came
from the East, and especially from the Mohammedan world, because the struggle was led and
continued by emperors who originated in the East

(i.e. Leon III the Isaurian 717-774 etc.). But the event which especially creates astonishment for those who study the history of this period and especially of the ninth century is the flowering which took place in all the phases of civilization. Whereas the human spirit was at a rather low ebb during the sixth and seventh centuries, now we observe a sudden reawakening with results which created brilliant achievements of the spirit. Thus, we see a flourishing of letters, the arts, and the sciences.

When in the year 843 the Iconophiles rejoiced over their definitive victory against the Iconoclasts, the spiritual revival which had been initiated did not stop. On the contrary, victory itself became the foundation for further fruition. A moving force of that spiritual renaissance was Patriarch St. Photios the Great.

This ecumenical patriarch and saint of the Orthodox East constituted a rare phenomenon and an enigma very hard to explain by the following generations. Being a man gifted by rich natural talents, and by cultivating these properly, Photios became the leading personality among his contemporaries in Byzantium, possessing an inexhaustible mind of creative thoughts for exploitation by succeeding generations. It is important to note here that his talents as a scholar, teacher, hierarch, missionary, diplomat, and churchman are not denied or minimized by any scholar of note. Although there is this basic agreement regarding Photios, there has been until very recently a very basic disagreement regarding his personal character, his holiness, and his contribution to Christian unity. Recently, however, new research into the life and times of Photios have shed new light on the subject and have gone a long way to correct the distortions and injustices that were heaped upon Photios by Western historians of the past.

Photios, like every great personality opening new horizons in history, became a sign of contradiction in his own time and in subsequent ages, because he came to be regarded as the instigator and the father of the schism between the Eastern and Western Churches. But before we present the opinions of past and of contemporary scholars as well as our own opinions about Photios' responsibility for the schism, it is necessary to present here a rather detailed biography of Photios, precisely because it is out of his actual life and his life circumstances that we can draw sound and valid conclusions about his real personality.

CHAPTER I

Birth and Origin of Photios

The extant sources do not provide us with precise information regarding the year of Photios' birth. It is generally regarded by scholars that Photios was born in the year 820 in Constantinople.[1] His father was called Sergios and his mother Irene. They both belonged to the most prominent families of Byzantium. The family of Photios was related to the Palace through patrician Sergios who was the brother of Photios' mother and who married Irene, sister of the Empress Theodora. Photios' father had a very important position in the Byzantine State; he had the office of Spatharios, that is, he was an officer of the imperial guard. Because Photios' family belonged to the part which favored the icons, it was persecuted by the iconoclast emperor Theophilos (827-842).[2] Thus, we find the names of his parents in

the Byzantine synaxarion and they are commem-
orated by the Orthodox Church as confessors on
the 13th of May.[3] Photios, in one of his letters,
characterizes his father as a brave, pious, and virtuous man by saying that he was distinguished "by
a richness of true glory and correct faith . . . and
by exile and martyrdom." In the same letter he
says that his mother loved God and virtue.[4] In
another letter which he sent to his brother, Tarasios with the purpose of consoling him on the
death of his daughter, Photios takes the opportunity again to refer to the glorious and brilliant
past of their parents by saying:

> "We must not betray our paternal exploits
> of fortitude, for they have seen deaths unlike
> those we know of. May we be spared from these;
> these descendants were separated by fire and
> water and, at that time bitter and heavy exile
> was imminent, and every deprivation of friends
> and relatives had been brought upon them, and
> they were removed from all those which bring
> joy, but they accepted all these with pleasure;
> and glorified God rather than those who govern
> the human things according to human minds."[5]

Besides his noble origin and relationship to the
palace, Photios was connected with the clergy by

a very important moral bond, because his uncle Tarasios, patriarch of Constantinople, (784-806) presided at the Seventh Ecumenical Council which was gathered at Nicaea in 787, and condemned iconoclasm.[6] In Photios' letter to a certain deacon named Gregory, we are informed also of the persecutions and the anathemas brought against his family and his uncle, Tarasios, by the iconoclasts: "Many years ago every heretic council and gathering of the iconoclasts had excommunicated us; not only us but also our father and uncle, confessors of Christ, and the pride of hierarchs."[7]

CHAPTER II

Photios' Education

It is very difficult to ascertain on the basis of the sources the exact conditions of the education of Photios and his brothers, Sergios and Tarasios. Therefore many opinions have been expressed. As was mentioned, Photios' parents were exiled because of their position against iconoclasm. Their children however may have remained in Constantinople, where they received an excellent education. But who were Photios' teachers? Who contributed to his outstanding education? Some scholars claimed that Photios was a self-taught man. He became an excellent scholar, a very keen philosopher, and a very profound theologian only after systematic and laborious private study. Others support that Photios was taught by the famous philosopher, Leo, the mathematician and archbishop of Thessaloniki, when he returned to

Constantinople and resumed his teaching there, after being deposed.[1] Whichever the case might be, the fact is that Photios had the opportunity in his youth to acquire a great deal of knowledge and to possess both ecclesiastical and secular learning.

Photios received his knowledge only from Greek sources, because he did not know any other language. He felt such a satisfaction and self-sufficiency with the Greek literature that he did not learn Hebrew and especially Latin, which was so important for his time.[2] Photios' excellent and perfect education became an event which was recognized by all his contemporaries. Friends and enemies did not hesitate to express their admiration for it. The biographer of patriarch Ignatios, Nicetas the Paphlagon, one of the most implacable enemies of Photios, had characterised him and his education in these words:

"Photios was not a man who originated from ignoble and insignificant people, but was from the noble according to the flesh and eminent man. He was esteemed for his wisdom and secular knowledge more than any other man who was involved with politics. He knew grammar and poetry, rhetoric and philosophy and also medicine, and every secular science in general

of his time. His intellectual superiority was of
such a kind that he seemed almost to surpass
his generation, and compete with the ancient
authorities."[3]

Thus it is clear that the admiration for Photios'
learning was common both to his friends and to
his enemies. As every adolescent and young man
is animated and possessed by dreams and desires
for the future, Photios, too, had his own personal
dreams. From one letter sent by him to the Eastern Patriarchs, we are informed that he was possessed by a strong desire for the celibate life, and
he never wished to become a priest. "When I was
still young, I wished very much to live alone."[4]
In another place, he emphasized his juvenile desire by saying that he never wanted to be involved
in worldly things. "In childhood I made a resolu-
tion to keep myself aloof from business and noise,
and to enjoy the peaceful delights of private life."[5]

We are informed, that during the ninth century
there had arisen a very strong conflict among the
Platonic and Aristotelian circles of Byzantium.
This is evidence of the spiritual uneasiness of that
time. Of this conflict among the intellectual circles of the Eastern empire we are informed by
George Hamartolos, who, because he belonged to

the Platonic party, said that Aristotle was an impudent and dumbfounded man, etc.[6] Such expressions enable us to understand the sharpness of that conflict. Photios belonged to the Aristotelian party.[7] Nevertheless, as the Greek historian Papparregopoulos, remarks, "Photios from time to time was illuminated by the brilliance of the Platonic ideology."[8]

CHAPTER III

The First Fruits of Photios' Education

Young Photios was the glory of his time, and his light could not be contained or hidden. He had to put it on the candlestand in order to shine upon others. Thus, before giving evidence of his philological, philosophical, and theological learning in the Church, he shone in politics. Therefore, during the reign of Michael III, courtier offices had been given to him which he honored. These dignities were *protospatharios,* officer of the court guard, *protoasecretes,* a diplomatic employee, and senator.[1] In the year 855, already a skillful and astute imperial politician, Photios was sent by the government to the Arabs in Bagdad as ambassador.[2] But all these dignities did not satisfy Photios. "I have been obliged to accept political dignities and secular responsibilities which

the emperor imposed upon me against my will."[3]
When Photios was able to isolate himself and to
find time to study and to communicate with those
who sought to find the truth, he felt untold ex-
ultation. Later, when he will be a "sign of contradiction"[4] with so much nostalgia, he will remember the quiet and tranquil life of study and
intellectual discussions with his learned friends!

During Photios' time, the progressive Amorian
dynasty (820-867) , which governed the Byzantine
Empire, took several measures to promote higher
education. Thus, during the reign of Michael III,
the experienced and progressive politician Bardas
decided to reorganize the higher imperial school
of Constantinople.[5] As a proper place for this
school the palace in Magnaura was selected. According to the historian Vasiliev,

> "Its curriculum consisted of seven main arts
> introduced in earlier pagan times and adopted
> later by Byzantine and Western European
> schools. They are usually referred to as the
> 'seven liberal arts' (septem artes generales) ,
> divided into two groups: the *trivium,* grammar,
> rhetoric, and dialectics, and the *quadrivium,*
> arithmetic, geometry, astronomy and music.
> Philosophy and ancient classical writers were
> also studied in this school."[6]

The clever Bardas, in order to attract many students to come to this school and to make education a common possession for both the rich and the poor, relieved all students from any financial burden. All financial needs of the school as well as the salary of the professors were undertaken by the Government. During Bardas' time and later, when the Government was assumed by the strong Macedonian dynasty (867-1056), this higher school of learning became the intellectual center and the intellectual heart of the empire. Anything spiritual great and outstanding that appeared at this time in the East was the product of this famous school.[7] Years before, Photios had already been appointed by Empress Theodoras' minister Theoctistos professor of philosophy in this school.[8] Now, with the reorganization of education and the war against illiteracy, Photios could not remain aloof. And as Vasiliev remarks, Photios at this time

"became the central force in the intellectual and literary movement of the second half of the ninth century. Exceptionally gifted with a keen love of knowledge and an excellent education, he later devoted his entire attention and energy to educating others. His education had been many-sided, and his knowledge was extensive not only in theology but also in grammar, philosophy, natural science, law, and medicine. He gathered about himself a group of men who strove to enrich their knowledge."[9]

Information about Photios' professional activity we receive from Photios himself, who wrote that he associated with those "who tried to be educated in the mathematical sciences and with those who tried to investigate the truth by logical methods, with those who tried to lead the mind to piety through the divine Word. . . . Such was the environment in my home."[10] As a result of his association with that scientific circle of friends came his early work *Bibliotheke* or *Myriobiblos*.[11] Together with his students, Photios analyzed and evaluated every kind of literary work. From this gigantic work we learn of the scientific interest of Photios and his students. Thus, in the *Bibliotheke* there are many works which come from the Gentile and Christian world and which are therein analyzed and evaluated, and whose contents are preserved in summary form. The importance of this work is very great, because in it we have valuable information about many works of antiquity which were unfortunately lost since then.[12] The loss of so many literary works which the work of Photios has preserved only in summary form may be largely due to the event that the transcription of manuscripts began at that time to be done in the new cursive script known as mind-form minuscule, whereas the older uncial form of capital letters known as majuscule was gradually abandoned and with it many of the older manuscripts.[13]

Another work composed by the young Photios is the Lexicon *Lexeon Synagoge*. Photios wanted to provide a work that could fulfill the great need for dictionaries. This work became an excellent aid for his young students. Maybe this Lexicon was composed by the students themselves with Photios' direction.[14] But Photios' fame as a great teacher and intellectual leader was not limited to the Byzantine state only. We are informed by Nicholas Mysticos, one of his students and later Patriarch of Constantinople, that Photios' fame and sphere of influence extended to the Mohammedan world. In an epistle sent by Nicholas to the son and successor of the Emir of Crete, he describes the friendship of Photios with the elder emir and says that Photios "knew well that although differences in religion are a barrier, wisdom, kindness, and the other qualities which adorn and dignify human nature attract the affection of those who love fair things; and, therefore, notwithstanding the differences of creeds, he loved your father, who was endowed with these qualities.[15]

The heart and the mind of Photios were so broad and spacious, that not only friends and enemies of the same religion, but also non-Chistians found friendship and understanding in him.

CHAPTER IV

The Ecclesiastical and Political Situation at the Time of Photios

Unexpected events came to disturb the fine and beloved professional work of Photios. The very commonly recognized, beloved and highly esteemed personality of Photios became the central point of struggle.

After the death of Theophilos (842), the imperial throne went to his six-year-old son Michael III (847-867). His mother, Theodora, governed the State until Michael's coming of age. After the death of Theophilos the iconoclastic party lost its influence, for the simple reason that Theodora followed the policy of respecting the icons. Theodora's close co-workers were her brothers Bardas and Petronas, her uncle Sergios Nicetiates and the most important and trustworthy of all, Theoctistos, who possessed the dignity of the Logothete of the Throne. Though all of Theodora's collaborators originated from the East (Paphlagonia), they followed policies different from those of the predecessors. They respected the icons.[1]

The first duty of the Government was the solution of the problems of the Church — to create peace in the State. Thus, by the deposition of the iconoclastic patriarch John Grammaticos and the elevation to the patriarchal throne one of the iconophiles, Methodios, the change of the Government's policy became clear.[2] Then, through the convocation of a holy synod and the restoration of the icons, it completed the victory of the iconophile party, which constituted the great majority of the clergy and the people (843). This event had such an influence on the Church and the people, that since then it was ordained that it be celebrated every year as the triumph of Orthodoxy against all its enemies on the first Sunday of the great Lent.

But in spite of this, namely the victory of the iconophile party, the desired peace did not predominate in the Church and in the State in the decades that followed. After a few years, the most important political figure of the Empire, Theoctistos, was deposed by Bardas' machinations. The economic robustness of the State, the spiritual renaissance which had brought peace to the Church and to the State, in a very large part were due to this strong and sensible political personality. The cooperation of Theodora, Theoctistos and patriarch Methodios, which gave so many fruits in every sphere, now was destroyed by the Bardas.[3]

In the Church, and especially in the monastic parties, there had been created a spirit of dissatisfaction with Theodora's government, in spite of the victory of the iconophiles party. This spirit probably developed because of the abhorrence of many monks, the so called "Zealots," to the renaissance of secular learning and the liberal and tolerant politics of the government toward the iconoclasts, who were not persecuted. Because of this situation, patriarch Methodios, though friend of the veneration of sacred images, had excommunicated the monks of the Monastery of Studion. However, he died in June of 847. Theodora, after Methodios' death, helped Ignatios to ascend the patriarchal throne. The new patriarch was a close friend of the monastic parties. Ignatios, who was to be the greatest opponent of Photios, came also from an aristocratic family. He was the son of

the prior Emperor Michael Rangabe and of Pro-
copia, a daughter of the Emperor Nicephoros I.
After the deposition of his father, Ignatios was
castrated against his will and became a monk. He
was a very pious man, a strict monk, and of a
very manly character. Certainly as a monk he
loved the monks and he was also loved by them.
As the monks were the vigilant guardians of the
tradition and claimed to conduct all the activities
of the Patriarchs, rejecting every "oiconomia,"
Ignatios also followed this line. He followed the
tradition and did not want to deviate the least
from the canons of the Church.[4] As is clear, the
occupation of the patriarchal throne by such a
man did not satisfy the liberal party and especially
the brother of Theodora, Bardas. He had deposed
from the administration the capable man in politics, Theoctistos. But Bardas could not counteract
this, because of Theodora, who favored Ignatios.
The rupture between the government and Ignatios came quickly. From 855 Bardas became the
closest co-worker of Theodora. From 857 he became the main regulator of the political affairs.
Because of his machinations, Theodora was compelled to leave the administration. She left the
throne to her son, Michael (842-867), who entrusted everything to his uncle Bardas. Theodora
and her daughters were shut in a monastery, and

Bardas sought to have them tonsured nuns by Patriarch Ignatios. But this action was against the
canons of the Church, and Ignatios refused to do
this. This was the first official cleavage between
Ignatios and Bardas. Also rumors circulated
among the people saying that Bardas did not lead
a moral life, because he cohabited with the widow
of his son. Ignatios believed those rumors, and
when Bardas came into the Church to receive
Holy Communion, Ignatios refused to offer it to
him. This behavior of the Patriarch greatly irritated Bardas, and therefore Ignatios' deposition
was decided.[5]

At this time in Constantinople, a bishop named
Gregory Asbestas was living as a fugitive from
Syracuse. Through his activity, his rhetorical abil-
ity, and his love for a spiritual renaissance he
almost became the leader of the liberal and progressive party in Constantinople. After Methodios'
death (847), he had been proposed for the patriarchal throne, and his elevation to it was expected.
Because of Theodora's intervention, it is said, Ignatios was preferred. Gregory's behavior toward
Ignatios was excellent. Though he was not elevated to the patriarchal throne, he wanted to participate in the joyful event of Ignatios' ordination.
However, Ignatios did not welcome him to offi-

ciate at the Liturgy with him. Gregory, full of indignation, threw on the ground the candle which
he had in his hand, and going out of the Church
he said that the Church got in Ignatios' person a
wolf and not a spiritual shepherd. The reason for
Ignatios' action was this: When Gregory was in
Syracuse, he had acted against the canons, because
he had consecrated a clergyman who belonged to
the Church of Constantinople as a bishop in Sicily, without the permission of the Church of Constantinople. During the years 848-854 Ignatios
convoked a synod and excommunicated Gregory.
This decision was confirmed by Theodora's government. These events strengthened the opposi-
tion of Ignatios. Furthermore, the hatred of the
"Zealots" against Gregory and his liberal friends
had increased.[6]

Photios did not participate in any of these
events. Certainly the immoral actions of Bardas
for the concentration of power in his hands, and
the forced and thoughtless actions of Patriarch
Ignatios were familiar, and surely they must have
evoked him in sorrow. But he maintained neu-
trality. He kept silence while studying, teaching,
and writing.

Because of these events, especially Ignatios' in-
flexibility and severity, and Bardas' absolutism, a

situation was created in which cooperation between Church and State was impossible.[7] Therefore, with Bardas' order, Ignatios was arrested and
was exiled to the island of Terebinthos (October,
858). He had been accused of treason. But according to the canons of the Church, this act of
Bardas was invalid, because Ignatios was not condemned by a synod. Therefore, he continued to
be regarded as the legitimate patriarch. Thus,
Bardas did not get away from difficulties. After
Ignatios' deposition, the situation in Constantinople is very unclear. According to historian
George Beck, the events might have taken place
as follows:

"Ignatius was prepared to resign under certain conditions. He declared that he agreed to a
new election, with the provision that the Patriarch elect should bind himself to recognize the
legitimacy of Ignatius' patriarchate, maintain
communion with him and respect his measures
as Patriarch. In other words, he was prepared to
recognize a successor who belonged more or
less openly to the monastic party. The search
for a candidate was not a simple matter, but
finally a compromise was reached and choice
fell on Photios."[8]

CHAPTER V

Photios' Election to the Patriarchal Throne of Constantinople

Regardless of how the events developed, the fact remains that Bardas did a great wrong to the Church with Ignatios' deposition. Therefore, because of the great injustice perpetrated on him and the honesty of character and power of Ignatios, the election to the throne of such a personality made it very difficult to reconcile the disagreeing parties and to drive out the impending crisis. But the cunning Bardas found the solution. And he found such a solution that good came from wrong he had committed. He recommended to the bishops the professor Photios. Then the eyes of all turned to the scholar Photios who had been neutral in the events that had taken place. Certainly, only Photios could calm the spirits and bring peace. The past martyrdom of the family, his relationship to the Patriarch Tarasios, the president of the Seventh Ecumenical Synod, his relationship to the Empress Theodora, who had been driven from the government, the possession of his office in the palace, given to him not by Bardas but by the deposed minister Theoctistos, and his fame as a virtuous and wise man became the reason that the enemies of Bardas, the Ignatian Bishops, agreed with Photios' election. Thus, in the gathered synod almost complete agreement of opinions prevailed and all decided to elect Photios. Even the five most faithful friends of Ignatios, after certain guarantees which Photios gave to them concerning Ignatios, recognized Photios' election and accepted him as legitimate patriarch.[1]

Until this time, Photios never had thought of leaving his studies and his other duties to enter the clergy. In the first letter he sent to Pope Nicholas I, he wrote among other things the following:

"I have never been so bold as to aspire to the dignity of the priesthood. . . . But I found myself attacked on all sides by the clergy and the assembly of bishops and metropolitans, and particularly by the Emperor . . . (who) acting in consert with the assembly . . . has given me no respite. The assembly of the clergy was large, and my entreaties could not be heard by many of them. Those who heard them took no heed of them; they had but one intention, one determined resolve — that of imposing the episcopate upon me in spite of myself. . . . The opportunity for entreaty being taken from me, I burst into tears. The sorrow which seemed like a cloud within me and filled me with anxiety and darkness, broke at once into a torrent of tears which overflowed from my eyes. . . . Those who thus did violence to my feelings left me no peace until they had obtained what they desired, although against my will. . . ."[2]

Also, in his famous second letter to Nicholas, he wrote:

"It was against our will that we were placed under this yoke. Therefore have pity upon us instead of rebuking. . . . We have suffered violence . . . we have been detained against our wishes, we have been watched closely, surrounded by spies like a culprit. We have received votes against our will, we have been made bishop in spite of our tears, our complaints, our affection, our despair. Everyone knows it; for these things were not done in secret, and the exceeding violence to which I have been subjected was so public as to be known of all. . . . I have lost a sweet and tran-

quil life; I have lost my glory. . . . I have lost
my precious leisure, my intercourse so pure
and delightful with my friends, that intercourse
where grief, double dealing, and recrimination
were excluded. No one hated me then; and . . .
I, accused, hated no one, neither at home nor
abroad. I had nothing against those who had
the least intercourse with me, and nothing a
fortiori against my friends. I have never caused
such pain to anyone as that I should reap out-
rage from it, save in those dangers to which I
have been exposed for the cause of religion.
Nor has anyone so seriously offended me as to
drive me to insult him. All were good to me."[3]

From what Photios says, one concludes that his
election became necessary from the situation; that
he was pressed by the government and the bishops
to receive the patriarchal dignity, and at last he
obeyed the entreaty of the clergy, people, and
government, and he accepted his ordination.[4]
That he was a layman was not an obstacle in the
Eastern Church. The examples of the patriarchs
Nectarios (381-397), Pavlos (686-693), Tarasios
(784-806), and Nicephoros (806-815) et al., who
from laymen received the highest episcopal dignity were living in the memory of the Church.[5]
Thus, in six days Photios received all ecclesiastical

ordinations. On the 20th of December, in the year 857, he became a monk; the next day, reader; the next, subdeacon, consequently deacon; then presbyter; and on Christmas day, he was ordained bishop. Photios received his ordination as bishop by Gregory Asbestas (about whom we spoke above) and by two Ignatian Bishops.[6] About his feeling before and during the ordination Photios says the following:

"I never aspired after this throne. Most of our present brothers and fellow-clergymen, if not all, know this well. . . . With many tears and with every delay, I came to this episcopal throne, because, on the one hand, the Sovereign at that time and also his ministers presented to me the implacable necessity, and on the other hand, bishops and priests, while I did not understand these things which took place. Thus, with common votes and common written decisions which strengthened the regal decision and confirmed the demand, they delivered me to the guard who watched me. And then, from that place and against my will, they have elevated me to this throne."[7]

With Photios' elevation to the episcopal throne of Constantinople, a new period opened, not only for the Eastern Church, but also for the future

of Christianity in general. "For the Church," says
the historian Ostrogorski, "this marked the opening of a time of upheaval, probably the most disturbed period which the Byzantine Church had
known. Photios was the most distinguished think-
er, the most outstanding politician, and the most
skillful diplomat ever to hold office as Patriarch of
Constantinople."[8]

Indeed, during Photios' patriarchate, the
Church was glorified. But it was also disturbed by
several conflicts. These certainly were not caused
by Photios himself, as we will see in the next
chapter.

CHAPTER VI

The First Patriarchal Reign of Photios

The wound which the impudent character Bardas opened in the body of the Church was not easily healed. In spite of the election of the best man of Byzantium, Photios, to the episcopal throne of the capital city, and in spite of the apparent calm, the crisis had not passed. Ignatios observed the events in silence. But when his adherents, bishops and monks, claimed that the newly elected patriarch could not have his own opinion, and that he should be just an executive organ of the dethroned Ignatios[1] and themselves, and when they found themselves before reaction coming mainly from the palace, they changed their mind. Two months after Photios' ordination, the extremist Ignatian bishops gathered in the church of St. Irene. They proclaimed as legitimate Pa-

triarch Ignatios and rejected obedience to Photios, depriving him of the right to officiate as a
clergyman (859) .[2] The situation was extremely
serious. Though in the past many distinguished
bishops and other important personalities of Constantinople had asked Ignatios to submit his resignation, so that the difficult canonical issue of
Photios' election could be solved, Ignatios refused
persistently. There are many scholars who accept
the fact that Ignatios resigned,[3] but many others
have different opinions.[4] However, the problem
which is difficult to explain for the scholars is the
sudden change of the Ignatian bishops. Professor
Dvornik wants to believe that "the reason for
this action may have lain in differing interpretation of the nature of the guarantees given by Photios to the five leaders of the Ignatian party."[5]
Certainly all these events were known to Ignatios
and obtained his approbation. Ignatios could not
tolerate the injustice which came upon him. He
did not have the spiritual power to imitate the
example of St. John Chrysostom. Therefore, because of his policy, he contributed to the deterio-
ration of the situation. When Photios was found
before such a revolution of the Ignatian bishops
he was compelled to take the necessary measures.
Now we can justify Photios for his reactions and
his denial to accept the patriarchal throne. He

foresaw the coming developments, and therefore, he had persistently declined his election. From this point on Photios' life will be one endless strife. Thus, Photios convoked a synod which gathered at first in the church of the Holy Apostles (859) [6] and then in the church of the Blachernae palace. With Bardas' demand, and to bring to an end the issue concerning Ignatios' resignation the synod decided against the legality of Ignatios' election, because he was not elected by a synod, but he was appointed by the Empress Theodora. Therefore, the whole of Ignatios' patriarchate was illegal. Certainly the Ignatian bishops, the monks, and the people who were under the influence of the monks protested against the decisions of the Photian synod. Then Bardas showed all his wild sentiments against the protestors.[7] Photios repeatedly protested against Bardas' barbarity against the clergy and the people. But animosities were found in both sides. What Bardas wanted to succeed had succeeded already, namely to turn the hate of the Ignatians against other persons. Thus, the Ignatians, moved by the situation and atmosphere which had been created were not fighting against Bardas but against the Church itself. Then Photios, full of indignation at Bardas' violence, and having decided to quit the throne if this situation should continue, wrote to Bardas:

"I knew very well, even before the experience of the prelacy, that I was unworthy of the episcopal dignity, or of the pastoral work. Therefore I was anxious, because they led me and they drew me to this hierarchical dignity. Would that death had taken me before my election. Because of this, I was grieved bitterly. I wept. . . . I was indignant, I did everything but agree with them, who elected me, and forced me, and I begged them to take away from me this cup of many and diverse cares and temptations. Now after the event, the events themselves teach me and censor my unworthiness. And fear no longer exists for the events which have taken place already, and I sigh and am perplexed for what has come upon me already. Because when I see priests, whosoever they may be, suffering all together for one fault, and being beaten, and suffering confiscation of their properties, and suffering humiliation and having their tongues uprooted (spare us O Lord, of our sins), how could I not call them who died more blessed than myself? How could I not regard the burden which they have laid upon me, as a censure for my sins?"

And after protesting against Bardas' other violence, Photios concludes his letter:

"These things I have written to you with tears filled with blood. As for you, then this is the first and last letter which you will receive from me. I write these things with God as my witness. If, in spite of my entreaties, you have as your intent to ignore me . . . , neither shall I write to you, nor shall I burden you; I shall retire from the episcopacy and weep for my sins."[8]

From these lines of Photios we are able to evaluate properly his piety to God, the gentle nature of his heart, which was touched by his suffering enemies, and also his generosity, which put his life in danger, confronting the irritable, omnipotent and cruel Bardas. After Photios' protest, the persecutions did not stop at a whole, but through Photios' actions at least they were mitigated. Ignatios, who was moved from the island Terebinthos to the island of Mytilene, through Photios' entreaty was given the permission to return to Constantinople, and his property was returned to him. Once again, efforts were made to persuade him to recognize Photios as his legitimate successor, but in vain. Ignatios was not persuaded. Therefore the problem needed a more general and more effective solution.

Thus, the Government and Photios decided to

convoke a new Synod, where Photios' recognition could be more triumphant and therefore he could without obstacles exercise his episcopal office. For the decisions of the Synod to have more value it was decided to invite the Eastern Patriarchs (those of Alexandria, Antioch, and Jerusalem) and the Patriarch of the West, Pope Nicholas I.[9] In his installation letter to the Patriarchs of the East and the Pope, Photios narrated the events which took place in Constantinople, and emphasized especially that he accepted his election and elevation to the patriarchal throne under great pressure.[10] Because of the conflicts in Constantinople, Photios was not able to send this kind of letter to Pope Nicholas I until the year 860. At the same time, the participation of representatives of the Western Church in the convoked Synod in Constantinople was sought obliquely. This Synod should solve the issues of Photios and Ignatios, and also the theme of the new condemnation of iconoclasm and other new heresies. The letter of the Emperor Michael III to the Pope also contained these same things. Nicholas I, was an ambitious and power-hungry man, who had as the purpose of his life to put the sovereignty of the Roman Church over the whole world.[11] Our contemporary Roman Catholic historian, F. Dvornik, believes that Nicholas I "is without doubt one of the greatest Popes of the early Middle Ages and the increase of papal authority throughout the following centuries is forever connected with the acts of that great Pope, whose writings on the sublimity of the institution of the papacy had an unprecedented influence over the canonists and theologians of the Western Church during the Middle Ages. He succeeded in bringing the whole western hierarchy under absolute obedience to him and he crushed all tendencies toward independence in the powerful Frankish Church."[12]

To such character therefore were sent the letters of Photios and of the emperor Michael III. Nicholas I, leaning on the power which he had succeeded in obtaining in the West,[13] regarded this as a suitable opportunity, since he had been waiting for some time to intervene in the East and to apply there also his ecclesiastical imperialism. But his dream, to impose his will in the East, was not an easy thing. His desire to make the Eastern Church the maid of his rule of the world was not successful, because the East was not on the same spiritual level with the western world. The West, because of its illiteracy, had long submitted to the papal claims. But the East, being the cradle and the mother of civilization and of Christianity,

rejected with great contempt the newfangled fabri-
cations and the distortions of Christianity created
by Rome,[14] as we will see afterwards. Thus Nicholas I, regarding as proper the opportunity for intervention in the Eastern ecclesiastical things, sent
as his representatives to the Synod that was convoked at Constantinople the bishops Rodoald of
Porto and Zacharias of Anagni. The papal delegation was ordered to examine the issue of Photios.
If they found that everything had taken place in
accordance with the canons, they were to recognize Photios as legitimate Patriarch, provided that
Illyricon and South Italy be given back to Rome.
These regions had belonged to Rome before 733
AD, when Emperor Leo III the Isaurian transfered them to the jurisdiction of the Church of
Constantinople.

In the Synod in Constantinople (861), Photios
was exonerated and Ignatios condemned. The
Roman delegation recognized the legality of Photios without enforcing Nicholas' condition that
Illyricon and South Italy be returned to him.[15]
Let us note that in an epistle sent to Photios before the examination, Nicholas called him the
"bishop of Constantinople" and glorified God for
Photios' Orthodox faith and his honesty of character.[16] This proves that the Pope was interested

in acquiring Illyricon and South Italy, and not in questioning Photios' legitimacy.

After the adjournment of the Synod, which has the curious surname First-second (Prima-secunda), the papel representatives Rodoald and Zacharias returned to Rome and made known to Nicholas the results of the Synod.[17] An envoy of the Emperor also brought to Nicholas the acts of the Synod as well as letters from Emperor Michael III and Photios. The epistle of Photios became famous for the ideas it contained. In this letter, Photios proves to be an excellent interpreter of living patristic thought, an architect of future Christian unity, an exalted hierarch and incomparable imitator of Christ, one who was able to find safe and immovable bases for the foundation and promotion of Christianity. In this letter, Photios says that the basis for Christian unity must be the basic dogmas of the faith and not the secondary and unessential issues over which Christians could have different opinions. And such things, according to the great patriarch Photios, are those which have been created by the different temperament of each nation, tongue, and in general by different traditions. Thus, the marriage or the celibacy of the clergy, the shaving or not shaving of the clergy, this or that kind of

prayers and fastings etc., all these should not be a
sign of division among Christians. Among other
things, Photios says the following:

"Nothing is more honourable and precious
than charity. This is the general opinion confirmed by Holy Scriptures. By it, that which is
separated becomes united and closely tied, becomes united more closely still. It closes all
doors to seditions and intestine quarrels; for
'charity thinketh no evil, suffereth long, hopeth
all things, endureth all things,' and according
to the blessed Paul, 'never faileth.' It reconciles
guilty servants with their masters, insisting in
mitigation of the fault upon their similar na-
tures. It teaches servants to bear meekly the
anger of their masters, and consoles them for
the inequality of their state by the example of
those who suffered the like with them. It softens
the anger of parents against their children, and
against their murmurs. It makes parental love a
powerful weapon, which comes to their aid and
prevents in families those strifes from which
nature shrinks. It easily checks dissensions between friends, and persuades them to kindly
the friendly intercourse. As for those who have
the same thoughts concerning God and divine
things, although distance separate them, and
they never behold each other, it unites them

and identifies them in thought, and makes true friends of them. And if perchance one of them should too inconsiderately raise accusations against the other, it cures the evil, sets all things aright, and rivets the bond of union. . . .

"It is this charity that has made me bear without difficulty the reproaches that your paternal Holiness has hurled at me like darts; that has forbidden me to consider your words as the results of anger or of a soul greedy of insults and enmities; that on the contrary, has made me regard them as the proof of an affection which cannot dissimulate, and of a scrupulous zeal for ecclesiastical discipline, a zeal that would have every thing perfect. For if charity will not permit us even to consider evil as wrong, how shall it permit us to call anything wrong? Such is the nature of true charity, that it will even regard as intended benefit that which causes us pain. But since there is no reason why truth should not be spoken between brothers or fathers and sons (for what is there more friendly than truth?), let me speak and write to you with perfect freedom, not from a desire to contradict you, but with intent of defending myself. . . .

"I hear it said to me: 'Men ought not to have

wronged you.' They say so to those who have
wronged me: 'They ought not to have done
you violence.' The maxim is excellent; but who
deserves your reproaches if not those who did
me violence? Who should be pitied, if not those
to whom violence has been done? If any one
left in peace those who did violence in order
to attack those who suffered it, I might have
hoped from your justice that you would con-
demn him. The canons of the Church, it is
said, have been violated because you were
raised from the rank of a layman to the highest office of the ministry. But who has violated
them? He who has done violence or he who
has been compelled by force and against his
will? But you should have resisted! How far?
I did resist even more than necessary. If I had
not feared to excite still greater storms, I would
have resisted even unto death. But what are
these canons that are said to have been violated? Canons never to this day received by the
Church of Constantinople. Canons can only
be transgressed when they ought to be observed; but when they have not been handed
down to us, there can be no sin in not observ-
ing them. I have said enough — even more than
was expedient — for I wish neither to defend
nor justify myself. How should I wish to de-

fend myself, when the only thing I desire is to be delivered from the tempest, and to be relieved of the burden that bears me down? It is to this degree that I have coveted this see, and only to this degree do I desire to retain it. But if the episcopal chair is a burden to you today, it was not thus at the commencement. I took it against my will, and against my will do I remain in it. The proof is that violence was done to me from the first; that from the first I desired as I do this day to leave it. But though some polite things had to be written to me, it was impossible to write to me with kindness and to praise me. We have received all that has been said to us with joy, and with thanks to God who governs the Church.

"It has been said to me: 'You have been taken from the laity; that is not a laudable act; therefore are we undecided and have deferred our consent until after the return of our apocrisiaries.' It had been better to say: We will not consent at all; we do not approve; we do not accept, and never will. The man who offered himself for this see, who has bought the episcopate, who never received an honest vote, is a bad man in all respects. Leave the episcopate and the office of pastor. One who should have written me thus, would have written agree-

ably, however falsely. But was it necessary that
one who had suffered so much on entering the
episcopate, should suffer again in leaving it?
That he who had been pushed violently into
that office, should be pushed from it with still
greater violence? One who has such sentiments,
such thoughts, must care very little to repel
calumny intended to deprive him of the epi-
copal chair. But enough upon this subject. . .''[19]

Pope Nicholas I, who regarded himself as Emperor of the entire world, did not take into con-
sideration the ecumenical Christian ideas of the
Eastern Church, whose best interpreter, at this
moment, was Photios. When informed that his
conditions were not fulfilled, he became exceed-
ingly angry, and his anger fell first on his representatives, whom he excommunicated. Afterwards, he convoked a Latin council (863) and
excommunicated Photios, using as a basis the
accusation that Photios had taken the patriarchal
throne uncanonically. He excommunicated also
bishop Gregory Asbestas, who played the princi-
pal role at Photios' ordination. Also, he threatened Photios, that if he would not conform to the
decisions of the Roman council, he would remain
in excommunication until his death bed.[20] Nicholas thought that he had before him illiterate Em-

perors of the West or toy Latin bishops who trem-
bled before his excommunications. He had not
understood that his opponent was the true tradition of eight centuries of Christianity, of which
tradition Photios was in full possession and its
defender. But Nicholas I did not stop at this point.
He wrote letters to Emperor Michael III[21] and to
Photios, furiously attacking Photios and not referring to him any more as bishop, but only as a
"very learned man."[22] He wrote also to the Eastern
Patriarchs.[23] In all his letters, Nicholas I openly
proclaimed the papal claims and did not recognize
Photios, nor the excommunication of Ignatios.

Then, Emperor Michael III answered the Pope,
saying that the papal decisions had no validity, because no one had appointed him and his council
as judges.[24] In his answer to Michael III, Nicholas I, repeated his claims in a sharper tone. He
based the Papal claims on the well-knwon false
documents (Constantine's donation and Pseudo
Isidorian orders) and on the Papal interpretation
of the well-known passages of the New Testament
(Matthew 16, 18, etc.) . He demanded that Photios and Ignatios be sent to Rome to be judged
by him. It is very clear that at this moment the
Eastern Church was greatly insulted by these un-
heard of papal actions. In spite of this, Photios

gave way to wrath and did not answer. He thought
that the only effective manner for the preservation
of the unity between East and West was silence,
because he knew very well that his words and his
letters would be in vain. The Emperor also did
not continue the correspondence.

In spite of the obstacles coming from within and
without the Church, Photios' Patriarchate gave
very rich fruits. Especially after his recognition by
the First-second Synod in 861, Photios dedicated
himself with zeal to the reorganization of ecclesiastical matters. As a sagicious man, he observed
that Christianity in the East was in danger because of the numerous non-Christians in the East,
North, and South. In the Balkan peninsula it was
necessary that the Slavs and Bulgarians, who had
lived there for a long time, should be Christian-
ized and become friends of Byzantium by every
means possible. It had been correctly understood
that the Balkan peninsula was the nerve center
of the life of the Byzantine Empire. Therefore, it
was inconceivable to allow freedom of action to
whatever other political or ecclesiastical power
which wished to enter the area. Thus, Greek missionaries sent by Photios and by the Emperor
under the leadership of the Thessalonian brothers
Cyril-Constantine and Methodios, came into Mo-

ravia (863).[25] With King Ratislav's cooperation, the Greek missionaries there preached the Christian faith successfully. In order that the mission might have more success, they preached in the Slavonic tongue. The Slavonic alphabet was devised by them to make the translation of the Bible and the liturgic books in the Slavonic tongue possible. Thus, the Greek missionaries did not have as their purpose the changing of the ethnic consciousness of the people, but their Christianization.

As a result of the success of the Byzantine mission in Moravia, King Boris I of Bulgaria desired to adopt Christianity. Thus, in 864, he was baptized and received the name Michael. The Byzantine Emperor Michael III was his sponsor.[26] Therefore, the Greek mission was free for missionary work in the Bulgarian nation. One of Photios' letters which was sent by him to the newly-baptized king is preserved. In this letter, Photios shows him what his duties as a Christian ruler are. We are able to see in it the excellent pastoral talents of Photios. Among other things, Photios writes to him:

"Your majesty and my beloved son, other graces bestow small and fleeting benefits. But those graces which help to improve the human soul, are the true graces, because they provide

great and immortal gains to the soul. The most
important of all primary grace is the correct
knowledge of our pure and blameless Christian
faith and the living of the sacramental life. By
means of this we led up sailed to the Triune
Deity and to the reality which is incomprehen-
sible in its essence to human reason and which
is the cause of all things. . . . This true leader
does not take care only for his personal salva-
tion, but shows the same concern and forsight
also for the people whom God had entrusted
to him. He invites and guides them to per-
fection in the knowledge of God. I beg of you,
do not contradict my hopes, but throughout
your whole life your behavior must be in accordance with your faith. . . . The Lord urges
us to present our virtues as fruits, and not to
disgrace our faith with our acts. Thus, we also
urge you and counsel you to adorn your faith
with virtues, and to cultivate the virtues through
faith that they may become more brilliant. The
ruler must have much goodness in all his actions, and propriety in habits. You must pray
alone to God. But you must watch against
slips of the tongue, because in many instances
a few words have wrought great damage, and
they sometimes subject life itself to danger. You
must avoid slanderers and accusers. . . . Do not

take friends quickly. And when you make friendships, you must make them only with those who are of the best character. Do not seek to hear pleasant things from your friends, but only true things. You must govern your citizens without basing yourself on might, but on their love. . . . Malice is a great illness for every soul, but it is greater for rulers. . . . You would be the best judge of others, if, when examining your own actions, you give an account to your conscience for your acts and devise ways for the correction of your mistakes. . . . You must remember always whatever good things others do for you, but whatever good things you yourself do you must forget them quickly. . . . The happiness of the subjects proclaims the wisdom and the justice of the government. These few words, out of the many things which I wanted to write to you, O true and noble child, to whom I have given birth with spiritual pangs, you must regard as divine contracts and as original models of virtue. And I pray that you present yourself as a living example of true and excellent behavior according to the will of God. For my sake, may you become a model and an example of piety and of every virtue, not only for your subjects, but also for your successor, an examplar for all mankind, and a great admonition and exhortation for every great and good thing.''[27]

In Photios' personality, truly Eastern Christianity during the ninth century had found a true pastor and teacher who was able to teach the evangelical truth correctly. Therefore, the brilliance of the Christian faith came forth from the Byzantine Empire successfully. The Russians, already after the year 860, came to Bosporos and threatened to conquer Constantinople. The destruction made by them was enormous. The inhabitants of Constantinople were terrified. They gathered in the city and were ready to defend themselves until their death. In this critical moment for the capital, Photios stood by the side of the people. Like his predecessor St. John Chrysostom, who preached the famous sermons ''against the statues'' for the consolation of the Antiochian people,[28] Photios preached to the people of Constantinople. Through Photios' activity the citizens were consoled and strengthened. But this first contact of the Russians with the Byzantines had after a few years very important results. Patriarch Photios tried and succeeded in the conversion to Christianity,[29] of the Russian nation.

Likewise, Photios' missionaries were working in many places around the Caspian and Black

Seas, where people of Turkish and other origins inhabited. These people were the Khazars, Alans, etc. The success of the mission there was very great.[30]

As we have seen, Greek missionaries were working in Bulgaria and Moravia very successfully. But the papal imperialism of Pope Nicholas I could not tolerate the developing brilliance of the episcopal throne of the New Rome, and its influence on other nations. The denial of the East to give obedience to Rome irritated him very much. Thus, in spite of his decisions and the decisions of his council, the entire East recognized Photios as legitimate Patriarch. He wanted to transfer the struggle to the dogmatic area, thus make Photios' annihilation easier. But Photios believed in the same creed as Nicholas. The latter then insisted on the return of Illyricon and Sicily to Rome. But as we said, Illyricon constituted for Byzantium the issue of life or death, while for Nicholas it was a theme of honor.

The already strained relations of East and West now began to deteriorate, because of the Bulgarian theme. The Bulgarian king, Boris I (Michael) wished to create an independent Bulgarian Church, while Photios intended to send only missionaries. And because Photios did not send him

a Patriarch or Archbishop, he turned to the
Franks and to Rome, and asked them for fulfill-
ment of his desire for an independent Church.
Furthermore, he asked the opinion of Rome
about different religious and moral questions
(866). Such an opportunity was just what Pope
Nicholas desired. Immediately, the bishops For-
tunatus and Paul, accompanied by other missionaries, were sent by him to Bulgaria. They brought
letters of Nicholas which gave answers to the
questions asked by Boris. Afterwards, Latin customs were introduced by the Latin missionaries
in Bulgaria who criticized severely the Byzantine
ecclesiastic customs.[31] Thus, the time came for
the confrontation between East and West, because, as we said above, the Balkan peninsula was
a question of life or death for the existence of
Eastern Christianity. Photios took the whole issue
in his hands. His silence did not produce fruits.
Rather, it was regarded by the papacy as a dem-
onstration of weakness. Having right on his side,
Photios sought and found the proper weapons
for confronting his opponent and averting the
danger which came from him. Photios observed
that if he based his struggle against the papal invasion in the Balkan peninsula only on the canons, the defense of the East could not be successful. Thus he transfered the defense to the area

of the dogmas and sacred Tradition. The Latins themselves gave him this opportunity. For they taught the newly converted Bulgarians hatred of the married clergy, fasting on the Sabbath, the performance of the Holy Sacrament of the Chrism only by bishops, the reduction of Lent to one week, etc., and further, that the Holy Spirit proceeds not only from the Father but also from the Son (filioque). This was a teaching which was until then unknown in the Church.

At once Photios sent an encyclical to the Eastern Patriarchs encouraging them to participate in the struggle against Rome's egotistical distortion of the true teaching of the Gospel and the Tradition. Among other things in this famous letter, Photios wrote:

"Impious and abominable men, men who emerged from the darkness (because of their Western origin), sprang onto the ones who were newly converted and on to the newly established nation, exactly as a thunderbolt or earthquake or a multitude of hail, and to speak more correctly, exactly as a strong and solitary wild boar. After they had divided the beloved and newly-planted vineyard of the Lord, by their feet and teeth, namely by their shameful

conduct and corruption of the dogmas (a normal thing to them), they have ravaged it. Because they have dealt craftily to corrupt them
and to detach them secretly from the true and
pure dogmas and the pure faith of the Chis-
tians."[32]

Therefore, the papal claims for primacy, the
insulting actions of Nicholas I and his council
against the Eastern Church, the issue of the papal
invasion in Bulgaria and the new teaching of the
Holy Spirit's proceeding from the Father and the
Son, became the basis and reason for the convocation of a Synod at Constantinople. Thus, in the
year 867, representatives from the East gathered
in Constantinople. From one source, we are informed that the acts of this Synod were signed by
one thousand members.[33] This Synod excommunicated Nicholas I, and condemned the Roman ecclesiastical customs and Rome's new teaching
about the Holy Spirit introduced in Bulgaria. Furthermore, the Western Emperor Louis II was
asked to intervene and to depose Nicholas I. But
during the same year, Nicholas I died, without being informed about the decisions of the Synod.[34]

CHAPTER VII

First Deposition and Exile of Photios

While the events followed such an evolution, and Nicholas I vanished from the scene of the struggle between East and West, new political changes took place in Constantinople. Basil I, the Macedonian, who was until now co-emperor with Michael III, had assassinated Michael's uncle Bardas. He then murdered his benefactor Michael III, and took in his hands the government of the State (September 867). To win the rabble, and especially the traditionalist circles (zealots) who were against Photios, and to earn Rome's favor — because Rome at that time was almighty in the West — he deposed Photios and elevated Ignatios on the patriarchal throne. To give legality to his actions, Basil decided to call a new Synod. To this end, he wrote to Pope Hadrian II, Nicholas I's successor, asking for representatives. Hadrian II sent as his representatives the bishops Donatus and Stephen, and his deacon Marinus. Hadrian already had condemned Photios and the Synod which had met in Constantinople in 867. Thus, the new Synod (869-70), which is regarded as the Eighth Ecumenical Synod by the Roman Catholics, condemned Photios and acquitted Ignatios and Pope Nicholas I.[1] Also, by this Synod the papal desires, namely the return to Rome of Illyricon and Bulgaria, had not been fulfilled. As we said above, the Bulgarian King, Boris I (Michael), had asked from Pope Nicholas I (866) the creation of an independent Bulgarian Church. But his wish was not fulfilled. Thus, at that time when the Synod in Constantinople (869-70) was gathering, there arrived the Bulgarian delegation, which asked the Synod to inform them to which Church their newly created Church belonged. In spite of protest by the papal delegation, the Synod declared that the Bulgarian Church belonged to the Church of Constantinople. Then Ignatios sent a Greek bishop, Joseph, to Bulgaria as Archbishop. Therefore we see that for the issue of Illyricon and Bulgaria, the Synods of both Photios and Ignatios followed the same line.

Though the Ignatian Synod (869-70) was constituted only of one hundred and ten bishops,
whereas Photios' Synod in 867 was attended by
one thousand, the deposed patriarch Photios did
not want to follow an irreconcilable policy and
disturb the Church. He took the way of bitter
exile. From his exile he did not send any letters
to his adherents to arouse fanaticism, but he coun-
selled them to bear the events without protest
and grumblings. Photios was not an extremist or
a quarrelsome man, but a peacemaker. As scholar
and a man of action who had been impregnated by
Christian teachings, he did not want to come down
to the mob. The papal delegation and Ignatians,
on the other hand, read aloud against him fiery
anathemas in the Synod (869-70). Thus, the papal delegation read the following anathemas:

"Photio curiali et invasori anathema.
Photio saeculari et forenci anathema.
Photio neophyto et tyranno anathema.
Photio schismatico et damnator anathema.
Photio Moecho et parricidae anathema.
Fabricatori mendaccorum anathema.
Inventori perversorum dogmatum anathema.
Photio novo Maximo Cynico anathema.
Novo Dioscoro anathema.
Novo Judae anathema."[2]

(To the politician and usurper Photios anathema.

To the layman and forensic orator Photios
anathema.

To the novice and tyrant Photios anathema.

To the schismatic and condemned Photios
anathema.

To the adulterer and parricide Photios anathema.

To the fabricator of lies anathema.

To the creator of perverse doctrines anathema.

To the new Maximos the Cynic anathema.

To the new Dioscoros anathema.

To the new Judas anathema).

Through his whole conduct Patriarch Photios
showed his great nobility, goodness, forbearance,
meekness, and aristocratic character. He was great
in theory and also great in deeds, full of love for
his friends and also forbearance for his fanatical
and malicious enemies. After earthquakes shook
the capital, many regarded them as coming from
God. Photios did not use this event to help himself, as the Ignatians had done before. Thus, he
wrote to one of his followers, deacon Gregory:
"Who are we, though we suffered so many unut-
terable things, to provoke such an anger of God,
to a densely populated city? . . . I ask, your holiness, not to think such a thing."[3] While in exile,

although he lacked everything, even his beloved books,[4] which could give him much comfort, Photios, did not remain idle. He wrote his work *Discourse on the Manichaen Revival,*[5] consisting of four books. Among the most famous of his works is *Amphilochia,* a "collection of works, in which topics of the Scriptures are discussed."[6] He began this work in exile and completed it later. Also, he corrected the works which his students sent to him, and added necessary observations.[7] Therefore, Photios was a spiritual shepherd and teacher during the bitter days of persecution.

Photios' peaceful and dignified conduct soon won the respect and honor of Christian society. Even his more fanatical enemies were impressed by his virtue and greatness as a Christian. Such a rare personality did not remain long in obscurity and exile. Emperor Basil I himself recognized the injustice and recalled his decision concerning Photios' exile. Thus, he requested that Photios come back to Constantinople and take care of the education of his children.[8] Also, after his return, Photios continued his teaching in the higher school of Magnaura. He forgot all the wrongs which had been done against him, opened his heart and asked Ignatios for reconciliation. The peace and progress of the Church was his first

duty. Also, Ignatios, as a moral man and a great
personality, in spite of his irritable character,
showed understanding and accepted the reconciliation. Thus, the two great men — whom the Orthodox Church recognizes and honors as saints —
forgetting the wrongs of the past, decided to work
together for the progress of the Church. After
the reconciliation came such a cooperation and
love between them that Ignatios often asked for
counsel from him. Photios writes concerning this
new friendship:

> "We tried every avenue for the restoration
> and growth of peace. We both fell on our knees,
> asked each other's pardon and forgave each
> other for any mutual offence we might have
> given. Later, when he fell ill and asked to see
> us, we visited him, not once or twice, but fre-
> quently doing everything we could to relieve
> his suffering. And if words could convey any
> consolation, this consolation, too, we have given
> him."[9]

As far as the relations between East and West
are concerned, the situation during Ignatios' patriarchate was no better than during Photios'.
Pope Hadrian II, when informed of the decisions
of the Synod of 869-70, namely, the subjection of
Bulgaria to the Church of Constantinople, wrote

to Emperor Basil I and to Ignatios protesting this decision. Also, with Hadrian's successor John VIII, Ignatios came in conflict over the same issue, because Ignatios remained faithful to the Synod of 869-70 concerning the church jurisdiction over Bulgaria. Thus, as we have seen above, Ignatios sent a Greek bishop to Bulgaria, and the Latin missionaries were expelled (870). Because of this behavior on the part of Ignatios, Rome was not any more satisfied than it was with Photios.[10] Furthermore, the strengthening of the Byzantine Empire in Sicily and Southern Italy, which came first through an alliance with the Western Emperor Louis II, next through the expulsion of the Arabs from Southern Italy, and thirdly through the expulsion of the Arabs from Southern Italy and the Slavic pirates from the Adriatic Sea, caused Rome to change its policy concerning the East. Thus, when Emperor Basil I decided to re-examine Photios' issue through a Synod, Pope John showed willingness and sent the bishops Paul of Ancona and Eugenius of Ostia to Constantinople. When they arrived in Constantinople they found a wholly new situation. Ignatios had died (877 or 878), and Photios already was on the episcopal throne, having been acknowledged by the claims and entreaties of the people.[11]

CHAPTER VIII

Photios' Second Patriarchal Reign

Photios, having been restored as Patriarch, desired to work again for the peace of the Church. Thus, in cooperation with the government, he convoked a Synod at Constantinople in the year 879, at the Church of Hagia Sophia. Almost four hundred bishops participated at this Synod. Because the newly-arrived papal delegation at the capital was not authorized by the Pope to participate in the Synod, Pope John VIII was officially invited by the Emperor and Photios to participate. John sent as his representative the cardinal Peter in order to join with the other two Roman bishops in Constantinople. The Roman delegation was authorized by John to recognize Photios. But Photios' recognition was only on the basis of the papal ideas about primacy. These ideas Pope John VIII expressed in the letters delivered to

Constantinople by his delegation. These papal claims were not accepted by the East at all. Therefore, the papal letters were translated into Greek, and all the sentences concerning those Roman ideas were omitted. Thus, the letters were introduced to the Synod in their new form. In these letters, the Pope recognized Photios' legality as Patriarch, condemned those prior synods in Rome and Constantinople which had been against Photios, and urged everybody to recognize Photios as Patriarch and obey him. Pope John wrote:

"Receive Photios, the wondrous and godly hierarch of God and patriarch, our brother and fellow minister, who is of like destiny and of the same portion and of the same heritage as that of the Roman Church. Receive him, not only for the virtue that he has, but also so that scandals may be taken from the midst and the peace and love of God may be planted in our midst. Receive him without hesitation or doubt, with love and faith. And cast out every poison of evil, deceit, double-mindedness and doubt, and receive him even as the Roman Church has received him. For, as we have learned from well nigh all of you, this man is adorned with many divine virtues, i.e., with wisdom and prudence as regards things human and divine, as well as with every other active virtue and dili-

gent care which have made him a laborer of
God who cannot be put to shame. We did
not judge it right to have such a man remain
idle and inactive; but, having been raised up
to the exalted position of your church and shining forth again, he should once again do his
customary deeds, which are pleasing to God, to
priests and to high priests."[1]

Photios was not moved by the Pope's highly
laudatory words for his person so as to be swayed
with respect to what John wrote about the primacy. He ended up deleting all references to the
primacy from the letters. Over all, Photios had
regard for the traditional truth of the Church.
Thus, the Synod of 879-80 did not become a papal
organ, namely a gathering where the Pope would
pronounce his decisions. The Synod, under the
presidency of Photios, and with free discussion,
decided independently of the will of the Pope.
Thus, Photios was acquitted, and Latin desires
concerning Illyricon and Bulgaria were ignored
once more. Furthermore the Pope's condition for
Photios recognition, namely that Photios ask par-
don for past events, was not accepted, because Photios did not consider himself responsible for the
past.[2] To show the atmosphere of that Synod, and
the feelings of the participating bishops, wequote
the following section from the acts of the Synod:

"How did Patriarch Photios reascend his throne? 'By the consent of the three patriarchs, at the request of the Emperor, or rather yielding to the violence done to him, and to the prayers of the whole Church of Constinople,' the Synod replied.

" 'What!' asked Peter (the Cardinal), 'has there been no violence on the part of Photios? Has he not acted tyrannically?' 'On the contrary,' replied the Synod, 'all took place with gentleness and tranquillity!' 'Thank God,'' exclaimed Peter."

After Peter's questions, Photios spoke in these words:

"I tell you, before God that I never desired this see; the majority of those here present know this well. The first time I took it against my will, shedding many tears, after resisting it for a long time, and in consequence of the insurmountable violence of the emperor who then reigned, but with the consent of the bishops and clergy, who had given their signatures without my knowledge."

Then Photios was interrupted by the members of the Synod, who cried out, "We know it all,

either of our own knowledge or by the evidence
of others who have told us."

"God permitted me to be driven away," continued Photios. I did not seek to return. I never
excited seditions. I remained at rest, thanking
God, bending before his judgments, without
importuning the Emperor, without hope or desire to be reinstated. God who works miracles,
has touched the Emperor's heart, not for my
sake, but for the sake of his people; he has recalled me from my exile. But, so long as Ignatios of blessed memory lived, I could not bring
myself to resume my place, in spite of the exhor-
tations and entreaties that were made by many
upon this subject."

"It is the truth," the Synod exclaimed.

"I meant," continued Photios, "to make my
peace with Ignatios firm in every way. We saw
each other in the palace; . . . He recommended
to me those who were most dear to him, and I
have taken care of them. After Ignatios' death,
the emperor entreated me publicly and pri-
vately. He came, himself, to see me, to urge me
to yield to the wishes of the bishops and clergy.
I have yielded to so miraculous a change, that I
might not resist God."

"It is thus," said the Synod.[3]

From the acts of the Synod, it is clear that the whole Church was on Photios' side. He was in the period of his glory and triumph.

In spite of the decisions of the Council, which created peace in the Eastern Church and unification between Eastern and Western Christianity, after a short time new obstacles came from the West. When Pope John was informed that the papal ideas concerning the primacy were not accepted, he was very angry. He protested against the changes of his letters in the Greek translation. But he recognized the decisions of the Synod. He refused to recognize only the decisions concerning the issues of Illyricon and Bulgaria. He continued to ask for the return of these two countries to his jurisdiction.[4] Later, this Synod of unity was forgotten by Western canonists. The anti-Photian Synod of the years 869-70 was regarded as the eighth ecumenical Synod, which Synod was actually condemned by the Synods of 879-80. This tragic error continues to be found today in the Roman Catholic Church, in spite of the excellent works of famous Roman Catholic historians such as F. Dvornik, and the condemned Synod of 869 is regarded as valid and ecumenical!

After the Synod of 879-80, Photios, being at the height of his power, was undistractedly dedicated to the reorganization of the Church. He made it a source of great spiritual strength for all human activities. Kerygmatic and philanthropic work took first place. His studies and the writing of new works, however, and his teaching to all those who loved education, were not overlooked. Now he was able to send his light everywhere.

According to F. Dvornik, Photios' relations to the Roman Church in the following years of his patriarchate were normal. Dvornik's opinion, however, does not represent the reality, because preserved information, regarded by him as fictitious, speaks clearly about provocation coming from the side of Rome.[6] We believe that the atmosphere was of such a kind that peaceful cooperation and harmony between Photios and Rome could not exist, because Photios' position concerning the papal ideas of primacy were basically in contradiction to those of Rome. Certainly Pope John VIII exhibited understanding and did not cut off Rome's relations to the Eastern Church, though it had not returned to him Illyricon and Bulgaria. His successor Marinus (882), who was a papal representative in the Synod 869 and was persecuted by the emperor Michael III because of his negative actions in the Synod, condemned Photios and brought back into validity the Synod of 869. After Marinus died, his successor Hadrian III (884) maintained a moderate position. Hadrian's successor, Stephen V, was full of arrogance, similar to that of Nicholas I and Marinus, and he restored the Synod of 869. He also sent a letter to Emperor Basil I, in which he expressed himself very negatively about Photios. The Pope's letter however, was not received by Basil, but by his successor Leo the Wise (886).[7]

CHAPTER IX

Second Deposition and Death of Photios

The year 886 was one of misfortune for Photios.[1] It began with the death of Emperor Basil I in his 74th year. The imperial throne was occupied by Leo, who had been, as was said above, one of Photios' students. Leo, for unknown reasons, after having shown great ingratitude to his former teacher, deposed him and elevated to the Patriarchate his sixteen-year-old brother, Stephen, whom Photios had baptized. Historians point to different reasons for Leo's act. Many say that Leo hated his teacher Photios. Others maintain that he could not tolerate the spiritual brilliance of Photios, which he thought would overshadow his own personality.[2]

After submitting his resignation, Photios took the way of bitter exile for a second time. He passed his last days in a monastery of the Arminians, whose exact location remains still unknown, studying and writing. He died about the year 891, far from the noise and the troubles of this world. The Eastern Orthodox Church soon numbered him among its saints. His memory is celebrated every year on the sixth day of February. This day is probably the day of his death.[3]

CHAPTER X

Photios and the Schism Between
the East and the West

Patriarch Photios, whose turbulent life we have seen briefly above, was a man devoted to study, research, writing, philosophy and theology. Against his will, he found himself in the midst of political antagonisms and conflicting human egotisms and animosities and, therefore, could not devote himself absolutely to his work to produce more. Furthermore, because of his vigorous reaction against Rome, he was regarded, and still is regarded by some as the father of the schism between the Eastern Orthodox Church and Rome. He was also regarded as the inspirer of reformers such as Luther, Calvin, and Melanchthon.[1] Photios' value as a great teacher, theologian, philologian and philosopher had already been recognized since medi-

eval ages.[2] But scholars studied Photios' works
from different standpoints. Also, philosophers and
philologists studied him through his philological
writings (*Bibliotheca, Lexicon, Amphilochia,*
etc.) ; theologians and church historians, studied
his theological writings and his position against the
egotistic papal claims of his time. Thus, to this
day, according to the opinion of many scholars,
we do not have before us a single work that pre-
sents the whole personality and activity of Photios.
Furthermore the basic disagreements between
Roman historians, who present Photios as an egoist
full of hatred and wickedness,[3] and Eastern and
other historians who present him as an excellent
and great personality, have made unprejudiced research difficult. The new researches of the late
Roman Catholic professor F. Dvornic and others,
who are moved by the spirit of contemporary
ecumenism, really have not given a full and true
picture of Photios' personality, because they want
to compromise the disagreements of Eastern and
Western Christianity. Thus, when the events
speak clearly concerning Photios' reactions against
Rome, which events explain his points of view
about the papacy, these scholars purposely do not
emphasize them, or they dispute the historicity of
the sources. In spite of this, the pictures of Photios'
personality is further rehabilitated in the West-

ern world with the passage of time. Therefore,
whereas previously he was depicted as one who was
full of hatred, an egoist, a liar, a father of division
and hate, he is now presented as a personality full
of love, forbearance, patience — a father and
model for future unity. Naturally, the different
opinions about Photios' character have a foundation on which they were based: because the Latin
sources contemporary with Photios' time and the
later Latin sources, together with Photios' enemies, the Ignatians, represent an evil and corrupt
Photios, whereas the friends of Photios and, his
writings and the events themselves, give a picture
of an altogether holy man.

We had the opportunity already in the above
chapters and notes to present the opinions of the
different historians about Photios' personality and
the greatness of his character. But concerning his
responsibility for the schism what is to be said?
The Greek scholar, A. D. Kyriakos, in an effort
to explain the cause of the schism and the strong
hate against Photios on the part of his contemporary enemies, namely Niketas of Paphlagonia
(+890), Metrophanes, bishop of Smyrna (857),
Stylianos of Neocaesarea, and Anastasios the Librarian, writes the following:

"The life of none of the ancient churchmen

has been so perverted by historians, as that of Photios. Nearly all the historians who have described the events which took place during the schism, were unfavorably disposed towards Photios, because he had fought their beloved papacy. Thus, instead of examining impartially of the events, they tried to present Photios as the cause of the schism, and to justify the papacy, following blindly what had been written about Photios by his avowed enemies, namely Niketas of Paphlagonia, Stylianos of Neocaesareia, and Anastasios the Librarian of Rome. The last was one of the most vile men of the ninth century, and therefore was condemned and excommunicated by three popes, because of his various crimes. . . . In spite of this, the Latin historians regard him more worthy of credit than Photios, who had described the events concerning himself in several letters, and more worthy than the testimonies of many Synods gathered in Constantinople between the years 867-879, as well as more trustworthy than the Byzantine historians who had lived after him, . . . namely Symeon the Magistrate, George Kedrenos, Zonaras and Constantine the Porphyrogennetos."[4]

Also, the Greek scholar George Kremos, who has written the history of the schism between East

and West, refutes the ideas of the German papist
Cardinal Hergenröther. In his writings, the latter
completely misrepresented Photios personality.
The historian of the Greek nation C. Paparrego-
poulos, was influenced by Hergenröther's works.[5]
G. Kremos writes:

"The Great Photios fell prey to the unjust
and deficient historical critique of Paparregopoulos of blessed memory. . . . Like an eagle
of great wing span, Photios flies above the
clouds, and at such a height, that the weak ar-
rows of the malice of the papists and the Greeks
. . . who were party to them, cannot even touch
the tips of his wings. Great men are beyond the
reach of the multitude and especially of en-
vious men . . . as the great historian Thucydides
says. . . . That which every foresighted, wise,
skillful general does to cut off every communication with the enemy on the part of suspect
and traitorous men living in his camp, and generally to obstruct every communication of the
enemies with his own army, to inspect the
guards, the sentinels and vanguards of his camp,
night and day, this also is what the great Photios did when he examined the dogmatic errors
of the papists. . . . If such a great field marshall
is blameworthy, then Photios is blameworthy,

too, as the choir of the papists . . . would have us believe."[6]

In general, the point of view of the East concerning Photios always was the same: i.e., that Photios was an excellent and full personality, and that he was not the creator of the Schism.

It should be noted that the schism did not come immediately in Photios' patriarchate. There were deeper roots and causes of the schism, for example, in the already existing difference of the spirit between Greek and Latin theology. Thus, the Greek fathers were occupied with the philosophy and theory of Christian truth, rather than with the earthly organization of the Church of Christ, as were the Latin fathers. Also, the alienation of the Eastern and Western people that sprang from the differences of customs, tongue, etc., came to be added to the rivalry and the hate which the Old Rome had for the brilliance of the new capital Constantinople and its episcopal See. The Ecumenical Synods, as is known, elevated the patriarch of Constantinople to the first in honor among bishops (Synods in 381, 451, etc.).[7] Historians even from before Photios' time find many schisms and conflicts between the East and the West.[8] But the most important reason for the division was and remains the papal authority and primacy which has been created by the Latins, who based it on false writings and misinterpretations of passages of the Scriptures.[9]

The Western tendency for innovation, and the creation of the dogmas unknown to the ancient Church, completed and fixed the schism. Therefore, when Photios, the scholar and great theologian, found himself before an unknown and crude Western theology, and before the papal imperialism of Pope Nicholas I and his successors, he was forced to fight them. Though Photios fought in a defending manner, yet he always extended a hand of cooperation and reconciliation. But he was never understood. Because he struggled against the papacy, he was hated and defamed by Roman historians.[10]

But the falsehoods, especially those of Baronius (1538-1607) and Hergenröther during the past centuries, have in recent years begun to collapse like paper towers. Regarding the research of the Roman Catholic historian F. Dvornik concerning Photios, Professor John Karminis writes as follows:

"After a long objective, impatial, scholarly investigation of all the problems concerning Photios, he (Dvornik) changed almost into an apologist and defender of him in many respects. He more than any other contributed to the re-examination of his history and to the restoration of the truth which had been so much perverted by the Cardinals Baronius and Hergenröther, whose erroneous opinion is repeated mainly by other heterodox theologians and historians."[11]

Professor Dvornik has written many works to show that Photios was not responsible for the schism. We find a resume of his studies in one of his works, which is as follows:

"Fortunately, in recent years new light has been thrown on the history of the unfortunate patriarch. Let us recapitulate only those discoveries which have been so far accepted by the scientific world. First of all, it has been proven that the second Photian schism never existed. The Patriarch Photius was duly and sincerely reconciled with Pope John VIII, and the Council of 879-80 officially sanctioned this reconciliation. Photius was never reexcommunicated by the Pope. On the contrary, when he was deposed by the Emperor Leo VI for political reasons, the Pope, Stephen VI, rose in his defence, and only entered into relations with his

successor, the emperor's young brother Stephen,
when the emperor sent him the copy of Photius' free resignation of the patriarchal see.
When Photios died, he was in communion with
the Church of Rome. It has also been established that the Church of Rome was well aware
of this reconciliation and that, to the end of the
eleventh century, the papal chancellery officially
recognized only seven ecumenical councils,
thus refusing to accept the so-called eighth
council which publicly condemned Photius in
867-70. The Roman Curia has not forgotten
that the decisions of this council were cancelled
in 879-80, when Photius was reconciled with
Rome, that this decision was confirmed by John
VIII, and that it was never afterwards revoked
by the Papacy. The Council which condemned
Photius, and whose decisions concerning the Patriarch were cancelled ten years later by another synod approved by the Pope, has never
since been counted amongst the oecumenical
councils in the Eastern Church. Nor can any
official decision of the Western Church be found
ordering this council to be counted again
amongst the oecumenical councils. This synod
owes the underserved honour of being counted
as the eighth oecumenical council to a singular
mistake on the part of Roman canonists of the

eleventh century, who found the Acts of the council in the Lateran archives and were delighted to read amongst them a decision forbidding the laity to interfere with the election of bishops. They were so delighted with this discovery that they not only forgot that this synod had been cancelled, but promoted it to be one of the greatest councils of Christianity. Naturally, when this happened the whole history of the Patriarch Photius was found to be misunderstood. A Photian legend was born in Western Christianity, a legend supported by the Acts of an oecumenical council, and which had accordingly to be believed without hesitation. This legend developed during the Middle Ages, and was codified by the first modern church historian, Cardinal Baronius, in the seventeenth century. These are the new discoveries concerning the history of the Patriarch Photius which have been so far in some degree accepted by the specialists. These new views are naturally destroying all that the Middle ages built up. If we look at the history of 'the Father of Schism' from this point of view, then naturally the imposing building which Cardinal Baronius erected in the seventeenth century and Cardinal Hergenröther so magnificently renovated in the nineteenth is cracking and collapsing before our eyes. The history of the great Greek has to be rewritten."[12]

Other contemporary historians also speak concerning Photios in a manner like that of F. Dvornik. Thus, in the year 1939, the Belgian byzantinist H. Grégoire, proposed at the Archeological Academy of Athens, Greece, a basic re-examination of Baronius' work *Annales Ecclesiastici*. He said that Cardinal Baronius had used erroneous sources concerning the schism.[13] Also one other Roman Catholic theologian and historian, Yves M. J. Congar, agrees with Dvornik's points of view.[14] Because of all the above reasons, F. Dvornik concludes his work *The Photian Schism* saying:

"We shall be free once more to recognize in Photius a great churchman, a learned humanist and a genuine Christian, generous enough to forgive his enemies and to take the first step towards reconciliation. On the literary and scholastic side, Photius has always ranked fairly high amongst those scholars who have studied his writings; in this field his name always commanded respect, as his contemporaries, friend and foe alike, unanimously testified. Scholars familiar with his literary work were not inclined to believe all the stories brought against him by his opponents; they were true to the scholar's instinct which prompted them to feel that a man who had spent his best days amongst books, in the company of the best representatives of the classical period and daily contact with many devoted disciples, was not likely to descend to such meanness and petty ambition as were imputed to him by his enemies; and it was a right instinct which led them to honour a scholar who has been prominent in transmitting Hellenistic culture to posterity."[15]

The Eastern Orthodox Church, remaining in its faith concerning Photios' holiness, and being thankful for Photios great and fruitful work for Christianity, reveres and glorifies him as a saint. The new Western investigations and the change of the viewpoints of the historians, especially of the Roman Catholics, concerning Photios' work and his character justify its traditional faith. Therefore, the Orthodox Church will never cease glorifying its chosen child, Photios, who worthily glorified it by his great Christian piety and knowledge, by his versatility and clarity of thought, theory and activity. And it will never cease to regard him as

"a champion of Orthodoxy, defender of the Orthodox, pillar and foundation of the Church,

an instrument of grace, chosen vessel, divinely-
sounded harp of the Spirit, fiery orator, most
wise hierarch, illustrious teacher of the world,
in word and doctrine, trumpet which proclaimed the procession of the divine Spirit from
the Father, even as the son of the Thunder
(Evangelist John) had spoken with divine authority, most steadfast adversary of the heresies,
censurer of the error of heresy, divine advocate
of Orthodoxy . . . most holy Father, great
Photios, illustrious in word and namesake of
light."[16]

SELECTED HYMNS FROM THE FEAST
DAY OF ST. PHOTIOS THE GREAT

(February 6)

Stichera

4th Tone: As one brave among martyrs' hosts

With inspired chants let us acclaim the great
Photios of holy fame, the all-lauded instrument
of the grace of God, the godly harp of the Com-
forter, the steadfast and most divine pillar of the
sacred Faith, the brave warrior and champion of
the Orthodox, the great teacher and hierarch, the
supremely blessed herald of true doctrine, the
staff and boast of the Church of God. With one
voice, all ye Orthodox chant with sacred and hallowed hymns, praising blessed Photios the most
illustrious, the whole inhabited world's great
light, the preacher of fiery breath, and famed
hierarch of the Church, the most excellent man
of God, the divine high priest, the wise pastor
and guide of Christ God's flock, Constantinople's
brilliant shepherd, the first in rank among patriarchs.

By a lawless decree, O Saint, wast thou torn from
thy faithful flock, and didst suffer grievously for
the blameless Faith, O radiant hierarch, most

glorious, blest Photios of great renown, firm foundation of the Church, steadfast pillar of piety. Hence, we honor thee with all zeal, O initiate and teacher, wise in Orthodoxy's doctrines, and far-famed herald of grace and truth.

Glory: Pl. of 4th Tone

Come, all ye faithful, let us piously acclaim most wondrous Photios, the hierarch and friend of the Lord. For, filled with apostolic teaching, and having proved a dwelling-place of the Holy Spirit through his virtuous life, he did drive the wolves far from the fold of the Catholic Church by his doctrine. Having set forth most clearly the Orthodox Faith, he was shown forth as a pillar and champion of godliness. Since, after death, he standeth even more nigh unto Christ, he intercedeth unceasingly for our souls.

Lite

1st Tone

Rejoice in the Lord, O Constantine's city, and every city, island and land, on this the august memorial of our common shepherd, the teacher and luminary of the Catholic Church, the thrice-blessed Photios; for in this life he struggled greatly for the Faith of the Gospel, casting down the haughtiness of heresy, refuting every error and censuring the lawless addition to the Creed. Wherefore, in the heavens, he enjoyeth now the precious rewards of his labors, and intercedeth unceasingly with Christ God for our souls.

2nd Tone

While acclaiming thee, the great high priest and guileless and righteous shepherd, the herald of godliness, the fiery mouth of the Spirit, we entreat thee with longing: Grant us a portion of thine intercessions, O Photios our Father, unto our souls' benefit.

Glory: Pl. of 2nd Tone

O man of God, faithful servant, minister of the Lord, man of aspiration, chosen vessel, pillar and foundation of the Church, heir of the Kingdom, peer of the Apostles, confessor and defender of Orthodox doctrine, refuter of soul-destroying heresy, O great Photios, cease not to cry out to the Lord for us.

Pl. of 1st Tone: Rejoice, thou truly fragrant abode

Verse: Thy priests, Lord, shall be clothed with righteousness, and Thy righteous shall rejoice.

Rejoice, O all-lauded hierarch of Christ; rejoice, adornment of the Fathers and Patriarchs. Both action and contemplation did cloth thy soul with their light, for thou wast a dwelling of unceasing prayer, a temple of gentleness, and blest virtue's great treasury; a keeper of wisdom everlasting and most profound and far-shining sun of discernment in things of God, mansion of peace and grace divine, abode of a two-fold love for both thy God and thy neighbor, delightful palace of humility. Entreat Christ the Savior that great mercy and forgiveness be granted to our souls.

Verse: My mouth shall speak wisdom and the meditation of my heart shall be understanding.

Rejoice, canon of true hierarchs and priests, the foremost teacher and instructor most glorious, the mouth of the Theologians of Christ God's One Holy Church; thou, in word and doctrine wast illustrious. O shepherd of great renown, the Apostle's true peer in life, eloquent preacher cutting heresy's webs in twain like a two-edged sword sharp with truth and the grace of God, instrument of sweet melody, and mind truly heavenly, most steadfast pillar of Christ's Church, the strength and boast of the pious flock. Entreat Christ the

Saviour that great mercy and forgiveness descend upon our souls.

Verse: The mouth of the righteous meditateth wisdom, and the lips of men know grace.

Rejoice, venerable boast of all priests; rejoice, thou comeliness of bishops and patriarchs, the Church's unshaken pillar and firm foundation and rock, hallowed spring of doctrine filling all with truth, exact rule of holy faith, wise expounder of mysteries, Photios our father, blessed staff and support of truth, man of excellence, bright with splendor most glorious, mortal attaining heaven's heights and angel dwelling on earth, light of the Orthodox faithful, axe hewing down grievous heresy. Cease not to entreat Christ in behalf of them that honor and praise thy memory.

Dismissal Hymns

4th Tone

Being like minded to the Apostles and a teacher of the whole world, O Photios, intercede with the Master of all that He may grant peace to the world and great mercy to our souls.

Pl. of 1st Tone: 'Let us, O faithful'

As a radiant beacon of wisdom hid in God, and a

defender of Orthodoxy revealed from on high, O
great Photios, blest adornment of the Patriarchs,
thou didst refute the innovations of boastful
heresy, O light of the Holy Churches, which do
thou keep from all error, O luminary of the
East.

Kontakion
Pl. of 4th Tone

With garlands of chants let us now crown the far-
shining star of the Church, the God-inspired
guide of the Orthodox, the divinely-sounded harp
of the Spirit and the steadfast adversary of heresy,
and let us cry to him: Rejoice, O most venerable
Photios.

Megalynarion

Rejoice, thou lamp of Orthodox faith and life;
rejoice, illumination of the nations that came to
Christ; rejoice, thou grace-filled beacon exposing
hateful error; O Photios, we the faithful bless and
acclaim thy name.

NOTES

CHAPTER I

BIRTH AND ORIGIN OF PHOTIOS

[1] K. Krumbacher, *Geschichte der Byzantinischen Litteratur*, München, 1891, p. 223.

[2] G. Beck, *Handbook of Church History*, edited by Hubert Jedin and John Dolan, Vol. 3, Herder and Herder, N. Y., 1967, p. 176; Migne, *PG*, Vol. 102, col. 877C.

[3] H. Delehaye, *Acta Sanctorum Propylaeum Novembris*, Brussels, 1902, p. 682.

[4] I. Valettas, *Photiou Epistolai* ("Photios' Letters"), London, 1864, p. 145.

[5] Migne, *PG*, Vol. 102, col. 972.

[6] G. Beck, *op. cit.*, p. 176.

[7] Migne, *PG*, Vol. 102, col. 877C.

CHAPTER II

PHOTIOS' EDUCATION

[1] G. Ostrogorski, *History of the Byzantine State*, New Brunswick, N. J., 1957.

[2] K. Paparregopoulos, *Historia tou Hellenikou Ethnous* ("History of the Greek Nation"), Athens, Vol. 3, 1932, p. 285; K. Krumbacher, *op. cit.,* p. 224.

[3] Migne, *PG,* Vol. 105, col. 509.

[4] I. Valettas, *op. cit.,* p. 145.

[5] Migne, *PG,* Vol. 102, col. 585B.

[6] Migne, *PG,* Vol. 110, cols. 128CD-129A.

[7] K. Krumbacher, *op. cit.,* p. 224.

[8] *Op cit.,* p. 285.

CHAPTER III

THE FIRST FRUITS OF PHOTIOS' EDUCATION

[1] Romily Jenkins, *Byzantium,* N. Y. 1966, p. 169; Enno Franzius, *History of the Byzantine Empire,* New York, 1967; K. Paparregopoulos, *op. cit.,* p. 286.

[2] F. Dvornik, "Photius," in *New Catholic Encyclopedia,* Washington, D. C. Vol. 11, col. 326.

[3] I. Valettas, *op. cit.,* p. 145.

[4] Luke 2:34.

[5] G. Ostrogorski, *op. cit.,* p. 198.

[6] A. A. Vasiliev, *History of the Byzantine Empire,* Madison, 1952, p. 296; cf. F. Fuch, *Die höhern Schülen von Konstantinopel in Mittelalter,* Leipzig and Berlin, 1926, p. 18.

[7] A. A. Vasiliev, *op. cit.,* p. 196.

[8] F. Dvornik, *op. cit.,* p. 326.

[9] A. A. Vasiliev, *op. cit.,* p. 296.

[10] Migne, *PG,* Vol. 102, col. 597C.

[11] Migne, *PG,* Vol. 103, cols. 41-1588, and Vol. 104, cols. 9-356.

[12] A. A. Vasiliev, *op. cit.,* p. 29f.; K. Krumbachner, *op. cit.,* pp. 225ff.

[13] N. Tomadakes, "Photios," in *Threskeutike kai Ethike Enkyklopaideia* ("Religious and Ethical Encyclopedia"), Vol. 12, col. 23.

[14] K. Krumbacher, *op. cit.,* p. 227ff.

[15] Migne, *PG,* Vol. 111, col. 37; A. A. Vasiliev, *op. cit.,* p. 297, and B. Bury, *A History of the Eastern Roman Empire,* London, 1912, Vol. 3, p. 439.

CHAPTER IV

THE ECCLESIASTICAL AND POLITICAL SITUATION

AT THE TIME OF PHOTIOS

[1] G. Ostrogorski, *op. cit.,* p. 195.

[2] G. Ostrogorski, *Ibid;* K. Paparregopoulos, *op. cit.,* p. 278ff; G. Beck, *op. cit.,* p. 175.

[3] G. Ostrogorski, *op. cit.,* pp. 195-196.

[4] Romily Jenkins, *op. cit.,* 169; K. Paparregopoulos, *op cit.,* p. 281.

[5] G. Beck, *op. cit.,* pp. 175-176; B. Stephanides, *Ekklesiastike Historia* ("Church History") ,Athens, 1948, p. 318ff.

[6] F. Dvornik, *The Photian Schism,* Cambridge, 1948, p. 18ff.; B. Stephanides, *op. cit.,* p. 320.

[7] G. Ostrogorski, *op. cit.,* p. 199.

[8] G. Beck, *op cit.,* p. 200.

CHAPTER V

Photios' Election to the Patriarchal Throne of Constantinople

¹ F. Dvornik, *op. cit.*, p. 48: "Having examined all the important accounts of Ignatius' attitude after his internment, we may then conclude with confidence that Ignatius was not deposed by force, but that he abdicated to forestall worse complications. His abdication was made at the request of the new regime, it is true, but it was acknowledged as valid and canonical by all the members of the higher clergy gathered in Constantinople, including Ignatius' staunchest supporters. Ignatius, himself invited his followers to accept the situation and to proceed to elect the new Patriarch." Also, on p. 53: "Thus consummation was due to Ignatius' wisdom in resigning and thus sacrificing his personal interests to those of the Church and to the new Patriarch's conciliatory spirit and readiness to make concessions."

² Migne, *PG*, Vol. 102, cols. 585ff.

³ *Ibid.*, cols. 593ff.

⁴ F. Dvornik, *The Photian Schism*, p. 50: "The Synod presented a neutral candidate, the protoasecretis Photius, the very man whom the Emperor and Bardas had in mind from the beginning. The choice, besides giving the government some satisfaction, rallied all the bishops present except five. Metrophanes, and no doubt Stylianos, were the most refractory. Why did most of the Ignatian bishops rally Photius? First, because he was a new man: though a sympathizer with the moderate party, he was evidently not numbered among its most outspoken members. His orthodoxy was above suspicion, since he had been persecuted by the iconoclasts; he was moreover related to Theodora."

⁵ B. Stephanides, *op. cit.*, p. 319.

⁶ *Ibid.*, p. 320. F. Dvornik, *The Photian Schism*, p. 52: "The fact that bishops of the Ignatian party took part in Photius' consecration is generally omitted by the Ignatians." Cf. G. Kremos, *Historia tou Schismatos ton dyo Ekklesion, Hellenikes*

kai Romaikes ("History of the Schism of the two Churches, Greek and Roman"), Athens, 1905, Vol. 2, p. 148ff.

[7] Mansi, *Sacrorum Conciliorum nova et amplissima collectio,* Vol. 17A, col. 421.

[8] *Op. cit.,* p. 199.

CHAPTER VI

THE FIRST PATRIARCHAL REIGN OF PHOTIOS

[1] K. Paparregopoulos, *op. cit.,* p. 291ff.

[2] G. Beck, *op. cit.,* p. 177.

[3] See note 1 of Chapter V.

[4] J. Hergenröther, *Photius,* Vol. I, 1867, p. 400ff.

[5] *Ibid.,* p. 327.

[6] G. Beck, *op. cit.,* p. 177. V. Grummel, *Les Regestes des actes du patriarcat de Constantinople,* Rasc. 1-3, Kadikoy, 1932-47, no. 459.

[7] B. Stephanides, *op. cit.,* p. 320; K. Paparregopoulos, *op. cit.,* p. 292.

[8] Migne, *PG,* Vol. 102, cols. 624 CD, 625AB.

[9] F. Dvornik, *The Photian Schism,* pp. 70-90.

[10] Migne, *PG,* Vol. 102, cols. 585-93.

[11] According to F. Heiler, "keiner jener Papste hat den Römischen Primatsunspruch 'in so stolzer und überragender Sprach' und mit so 'formaler Volendung und Präzision' ausgesprochen wie Nikolaus I." Therefore, "durch Nikolaus I wurde das römische Papstum tatsächlich zum Weltimperium, zur 'pontifikalen Theokratie.'" Nicholas "totius mundi imperatorem se fecit," as if he was "imperator-pontifex" and "geistlicher Imperator" and "dominus orbis terarum." (*Altkirchliche Autonomie und päpstlicher Zentralismus,* München,

1941, pp. 239, 240, 242). The contemporary of Nicholas I,
Regimus, says the following describing this Pope: "Post bea-
tum Gregorium usque in praesens nullus in Romana urbe illi
videtur aequi parandus; regimus ac tyrannis imperavit, eisque
ac si Dominus orbis terarrum auctoritate praefuit" (I. Valettas,
op. cit., p. 43; cf. I. Karmires, *Dyo Byzantinoi Hierarchai kai
to Schisma tes Romaikes Ekklesias* ("Two Byzantine Hierarchs and the Schism of the Roman Church"), Athens, 1950,
pp. 105-106).

[12] "The Patriarch Photius, Father of the Schism or Patron
of Reunion?" in report of the *Proceedings at the Church
Unity Octave*, Oxford, 1942, p. 24.

[13] I. Karmires, *op. cit.*, p. 106ff.

[14] S. Bilales, *Orthodoxia kai Papismos* ("Orthodoxy and
Papism"), Vol. 1, Athens, 1969, pp. 207-223.

[15] B. Stephanides, *op. cit.*, p. 320ff; G. Beck *op. cit.*, p.
178ff.

[16] Migne, *PL*, Vol. 119, col. 780.

[17] F. Dvornik, *op. cit.*, p. 91ff.

[18] Migne, *PG*, Vol. 102, cols. 593-617.

[19] *Narrationis ordo de Photti repulsione Epistolae* VI,
556-61, G. Ostrogorski, *op. cit.*, p. 200.

[20] Migne, *PL*, Vol. 3, cols. 790-794.

[21] Migne, *PL*, Vol. 3, cols. 785-790.

[22] Migne, *PL*, Vol. 7, cols. 783-785.

[23] B. Stephanides, *op. cit.*, p. 223.

[24] G. Ostrogorski, *op. cit.*, p. 202.

[25] *Ibid.*, pp. 204-205.

[26] I. Valettas, *op. cit.*, pp. 200-248. The original Greek text
is in Migne, *PG*, Vol. 102, cols. 628-96.

[27] Migne, *PG,* Vols. 15-222.

[28] G. Ostrogorski, *op. cit.,* p. 202-03; Migne, *PG,* Vol. 102, col. 736f.

[29] G. Ostrogorski, *op. cit.,* p. 203.

[30] B. Stephanides, *op. cit.,* p. 325; G. Beck, *op. cit.,* p. 179ff; K. Paparregopoulos, *op. cit.,* p. 300ff; G. Ostrogorski, *op. cit.,* p. 204ff; A. A. Vasiliev, *op. cit.,* p. 290.

[31] Migne, *PG,* Vol. 102, col. 724BC. See also Chrysostomos Papadopoulos, *He Ekklesia tes Boulgarias* ("The Church of Bulgaria"), Athens, 1957, p. 34ff. In the letter which he sent to the Bulgarian King Boris I (Michael) Pope Jonh VIII says against the Greeks the following: "Everyday they are confounded by new and different teachings and doctrines" (Mansi, *op. cit.,* Vol. 17A, col. 119). And in another place: "We are grieved and we lament, worrying and fearing lest, if you by chance follow the Greeks, since they have fallen into various heresies and schisms in their usual way, you also with them (fall into) the depths of error. For I ask you son with the words of Moses 'ask your father and he will announce to you, ask your elders and they will say unto you,' if ever the Greeks have been free from this or that heresy" (*Ibid.,* p. 62).

[32] B. Stephanides, *op. cit.,* p. 325.

[33] *Ibid.,* p. 327.

CHAPTER VII

First Deposition and Exile of Photios

[1] F. Dvornik, *The Photian Schism,* pp. 132-57; G. Beck, *op. cit.,* p. 181; G. Ostrogorski, *op. cit.,* p. 207ff; B. Stephanides, *op. cit.,* p. 327ff; A. A. Vasiliev, *op. cit.,* p. 330ff.

[2] Migne, *PL,* Vol. 129, col. 118C.

[3] Migne, *PG,* Vol. 102, col. 873D.

[4] *Ibid.,* col. 765Df.

[5] *Ibid.,* cols. 16-264.

[6] K. Krumbacher, *op. cit.,* p. 229.

[7] Migne, *PG,* Vol. 102, cols. 857B, 901DC, 904ABC, 908, etc.

[8] F. Dvornik, *The Photian Schism,* p. 164, G. Ostrogorski, *op. cit.,* p. 212.

[9] Mansi, *op. cit.,* col. 484.

[10] F. Dvornik, *op. cit.,* p. 136 writes on this: "Pope Hadrian had acknowledged Ignatius as the legitimate Patriarch, on condition that he should undertake nothing contrary to Roman interests in Bulgaria; that, should he be daring enough to so do, he would be severed from communion with Rome, and therefore be excommunicated. In no other sense could these words of John VIII be explained. We therefore have here indisputable evidence that the Bulgarian issue played a leading part in all dealings with Photios by Nicholas, since his successor makes his recognition of Ignatios conditional on the latter's attitude towards Roman interests in Bulgaria. This condition was laid down in the letter which the legates handed to Ignatios at the time of the conference that met after the Ignatian Synod to settle Bulgaria's fate; and the legates were not to produce the letter, except in the urgent case of Roman interests being actually at stake.

This helps us to explain the enigmatic passage in the Pope's letter to Domagoi, referring to Ignatios as having been repeatedly excommunicated as a result of these offenses. If Ignatios' recognition by Hadrian had been made to depend on his attitude towards Bulgaria, and if the Patriarch had been threatened with excommunication if ever he dared to trespass on Roman rights in Bulgaria, then John could treat Ignatios as excommunicated, as soon as it became clear that Ignatios had failed to observe the condition. Yet, on the other hand, because John VIII did not wish to close the door to a possible settlement, he put off passing public sentence on Ignatios as long as there remained the least hope of the Patriarch acknowledging his fault. He must therefore have twice appealed to him before the last summons, the only one attested by a papal letter. It is worded in very resolute terms: Ignatios will be excommunicated, if he does not recall the Greek priests from Bulgaria within 30 days. In another letter to the Greek clergy of the same country, the Pope confirmed the sentence of excommunication once pronounced against them by Hadrian. But should the bishops and priests not quit Bulgarian territory within a month, they would all be suspended and excommunicated." See also G. Every, *The Byzantine Patriarchate 451-1204,* London, 1947, p. 126f.

[11] *Ibid.,* pp. 159-201; B. Stephanides, *op. cit.,* p. 332ff; A. A. Vasiliev, *op. cit.,* p. 330; G. Beck, *op. cit.,* p. 184ff.

CHAPTER VIII

PHOTIOS' SECOND PATRIARCHAL REIGN

[1] Mansi, col. 396ff.

[2] G. Gill, *The Council of Florence,* p. 3, 4. Cf. S. Bilales, *op. cit.,* p. 216f.

[3] Mansi, col. 484. See also A. Guettée, *The Papacy,* New York, pp. 321-22.

[4] B. Stephanides, *op. cit.,* p. 336; G. Beck, *op. cit.,* p. 187.

[5] F. Dvornik, *The Photian Schism,* p. 202f.

[6] J. Hergenröther, *Photius,* Vol. II, 1867, pp. 571-78. See also B. Stephanides, *op. cit.,* p. 336f.

[7] F. Dvornik, *op. cit.,* p. 215f; B. Stephanides, *op. cit.,* p. 337f; G. Beck, *op cit.,* p. 187f.

CHAPTER IX

SECOND DEPOSITION AND DEATH OF PHOTIOS

[1] F. Dvornik, *op. cit.,* p. 237ff.

[2] G. Ostrogorski, *op. cit.,* p. 215; F. Kattenbush in *Herzog-Hauck, Realencyklopädie,* Vol. 15, 1904, p. 385; J. Hergenröther, *op. cit.,* Vol. II, 1867, pp. 668f, 672f.

[3] N. Tomadakes, *op. cit.*, col. 27; K. Krumbacher, *op. cit.*, p. 225; G. Beck, *op. cit.*, p. 188.

CHAPTER X

PHOTIOS AND THE SCHISM BETWEEN
THE EAST AND THE WEST

[1] F. Dvornik, *op. cit.*, p. 1: "Photius is stated to have inspired Luther, Calvin, Melanchthon and other famous reformers in launching their campaigns against the Papacy and its authority."

[2] N. Tomadakes, *op. cit.*, p. 27.

[3] F. Dvornik, *op. cit.*, p. 4: "Blinded (so it is alleged) by pride and lust for power, Photius tried to obtain recognition from Nicholas I by misrepresenting the circumstances of his installation in Constantinople, but the Pope, duly informed by Ignatius' envoys of the true state of things, refused to recognize a Patriarch who had raised himself to the dignity in total disregard of canonical precedent. Photius, without taking any notice of the sentence, summoned a synod of the Eastern Church, deposed the Pope and created the 'first great Schism.' Not until the pious Emperor Basil I had murdered the iniquitous Emperor Michael III, whose reign was execrated by the whole of Byzantium, did Photius receive his punishment; then he was dethroned and solemnly condemned by the Eighth Oecumenical Council (869-70), that favourite source in the medieval canonical legislation of the West. But Photius insinuated himself once more into the Emperor's favour and, after Ignatius' death reoccupied the patriarchal throne; to make sure this time of papal approval, he received the Pope, who was willing on certain conditions to show leniency, by falsifying his letters and also those sent by the Pope to the Emperor and the Fathers of a Council summoned to examine his case. He bribed the legates sent by the Pope and tampered with the Acts of the Council. When John VIII learned that he had been hoodwinked by the astute Greek, he forthwith excommu-

nicated him. Hence arose the second schism, which was to last
till the end of the ninth century and to cast its shadow over
the tenth; finally there came the great rapture of 1054 between
East and West, the rift that has withstood all attempts at heal-
ing and has been such a disaster to Christendom. This was
the kind of picture which has generally been accepted as au-
thentic in the West."

⁴ A. D. Kyriakos, *Antipapika* ("Against the Papacy"), Vol.
I, Athens, 1893, pp. 51, 52. Cf. S. Bilales, *op. cit.,* p. 218.

⁵ K. Paparregopoulos, *op. cit.,* Vol. V, Athens, 1932, p.
264ff.

⁶ G. Kremos, *op. cit.,* Vol. II, pp. 412, 413, 416.

⁷ I. Karmires, *op. cit.,* p. 73ff.

⁸ See Kremos for the Orthodox point of view *op. cit.,* pp.
493-95. For the Roman Catholic point of view, see M. Jugie,
Le Schisme Byzantin, Paris, 1941, p. 9.

⁹ Matthew 16:16-19; Luke 9:18-21; John 21:15ff.

¹⁰ F. Dvornik, *op. cit.,* p. 1: "Few names in the history of
Christianity have inspired feelings so conflicting as that of the
Greek Patriarch Photius. Saint and hero in the eyes of the
Christian East, he is branded by the Christian West as the
man who unbolted the safeguards of unity and let loose
the disruptive forces of dissent and schism. Whilst the East
invokes his name as one that carries weight with God, the
West still quotes it as the symbol of pride and lust for ecclesiastical domination, hailed by all who ever claimed a larger
share for nationalism in the life of the Church and a closer
association between man and God, it is reprobated by others
as the badge of disruption and an element destructive of Christian univerality."

¹¹ I. Karmires, *op. cit.,* p. 57.

¹² F. Dvornik, "The Patriarch Photius, Father of Schism or
Patron of Reunion?" in *Report of the Proceedings at the
Church Unity Octave,* Oxford, 1942, pp. 20-21.

[13] F. Dvornik, *op. cit.*, p. 12; S. Bilales, *op. cit.*, p. 220.

[14] Yves M. J. Congar, *Chrétiens en Dialogue*, Paris, 1964, p. 49.

[15] p. 432f.

[16] I. Karmires, *op. cit.*, p. 65.

SELECTED BIBLIOGRAPHY

Beck, G. H., *Kirche und Theologische Literatur im Byzantinischen Reich,* München, 1959.

Bilales, Sp. Spyridon, *Orthodoxia kai Papismos* ("Orthodoxy and Papacy"), Vol. I, Athens, 1969.

Bury, J. B., "The Relationship of Photius to the Empress Theodora," in *English Historical Review* (1890), pp. 255-58.

————. *The Imperial Administrative System in the Ninth Century,* London, 1911.

Caspar, E., *Geschichte des Papstums,* Tübingen, 1930, 1933.

Congar, J. M. Yves, *Chrétiens en Dialogue, contributions Catholiques a l' Oecumenisme,* Paris, 1964.

Dvornik, F., "Rome and Constantinople in the Ninth Century," in *Eastern Churches Quarterly,* 1939.

————. "The Patriarch Photius, Father of Schism or Patron of Reunion?" in *Report of the Proceedings at the Church Unity Octave,* Oxford, 1942.

————. "Patriarch Photius, Scholar and Statesman," *Classical Folia,* 13 (1959), 3-18; 14 (1960), 3-22.

————. The Photian Schism, Cambridge, 1948.

Haller, J., *Das Papstum. Idee und Wirklichkeit,* Stuttgart, 1934.

————. *Nikolaus I und Pseudo-Isid.,* Stuttgart, 1936.

Heiler, F., *Altkirchliche Autonomie und päpstlicher Zentralisnus,* München, 1941.

Hergenröther, J., *Photius, Patriarch von Konstantinople,* 5 vols., Regensburg, 1967-9.

Jedin, Hubert, *Handbuch der Kirchengeschichte,* III/I, Freiburg-Basel-Wien, 1966. (Transl. into English by A. Biggs, *Handbook of Church History,* III, N. Y. 1969.)

Kalivas, Christophoros, *Papikos Holoklerotismos* ("Papal Totalitarianism"), Athens, 1964.

Karmires, Ioannes, *Dyo Byzantinoi Hierarchai kai to Schisma tes Romaikes Ekklesias* ("Two Byzantine Hierarchs and the Schism of the Roman Church"), Athens, 1950.

Kremos, P. G., *Historia tou Schismatos ton dyo Ekklesion, Hellenikes kai Romaikes* ("History of the Schism of the two Churches, Greek and Roman"), Vol. I, Athens, 1905, Vol. II, 1907.

Krumbacher, K., *Geschichte der Byzantinischen Litteratur von Justinian bis zum Ende des oströmischen Reiches* (527-1453), München, 1897; reprinted, 2 vols., N. Y. 1958.

Ostrogorski, G., *Studien zur Geschichte der Byzantinischen Bilderstreites*, Breslau, 1929.

Papadopoulos, Chysostomos, *To Proteion tou Episkopou Romes, Historike kai Kritike Melete* ("The Primacy of the Bishop of Rome, A Historical and Critical Study") Athens, 1930.

————. *He Ekklesia tes Boulgarias* ("The Church of Bulgaria"), Athens, 1957.

Paparregopoulos, K., *Historia tou Hellenikou Ethnous* ("History of the Greek Nation"), Vol. III, Athens, 1887.

Runciman, S., *The Eastern Schism*, Oxford, 1955.

Stephanides, B., "Nea Hermeneia tou Onomatos tes Protodeuteras Synodou tou 861" (New Definition of the Name of the First-Second Council of 861), in *Ekklesia*, 1947, p. 132ff.

————. *Ekklesiastike Historia* ("Church History"), Athens, 1959.

Trempelas, P., *Peri to Proteion tou Episkopou Romes* ("Concerning the Primacy of the Bishop of Rome"), Athens, 1965.

Vasiliev, A. A., *History of the Byzantine Empire*, 2 vols., Madison, 1961.

INDEX